enVision® Mathematics

Common Core

Volume 2 Topics 9-14

Authors

Randall I. Charles
Professor Emeritus
Department of Mathematics
San Jose State University
San Jose, California

Jennifer Bay-Williams
Professor of Mathematics Education
College of Education and Human
Development
University of Louisville
Louisville, Kentucky

Robert Q. Berry, III
Professor of Mathematics Education
Department of Curriculum,
Instruction and Special Education
University of Virginia
Charlottesville, Virginia

Janet H. Caldwell
Professor Emerita
Department of Mathematics
Rowan University
Glassboro, New Jersey

Zachary Champagne
Assistant in Research
Florida Center for Research in Science,
Technology, Engineering, and
Mathematics (FCR-STEM)
Jacksonville, Florida

Juanita Copley
Professor Emerita, College of Education
University of Houston
Houston, Texas

Warren Crown
Professor Emeritus of Mathematics
Education
Graduate School of Education
Rutgers University
New Brunswick, New Jersey

Francis (Skip) Fennell
Professor Emeritus of
Education and Graduate and
Professional Studies
McDaniel College
Westminster, Maryland

Karen Karp
Professor of Mathematics Education
School of Education
Johns Hopkins University
Baltimore, Maryland

Stuart J. Murphy
Visual Learning Specialist
Boston, Massachusetts

Jane F. Schielack
Professor Emerita
Department of Mathematics
Texas A&M University
College Station, Texas

Jennifer M. Suh
Associate Professor for
Mathematics Education
George Mason University
Fairfax, Virginia

Jonathan A. Wray
Mathematics Supervisor
Howard County Public Schools
Ellicott City, Maryland

SAVVAS
LEARNING COMPANY

Mathematicians

Roger Howe
Professor of Mathematics
Yale University
New Haven, Connecticut

Gary Lippman
Professor of Mathematics and
Computer Science
California State University, East Bay
Hayward, California

ELL Consultants

Janice R. Corona
Independent Education Consultant
Dallas, Texas

Jim Cummins
Professor
The University of Toronto
Toronto, Canada

Reviewers

Katina Arnold
Teacher
Liberty Public School District
Kansas City, Missouri

Christy Bennett
Elementary Math and Science
Specialist
DeSoto County Schools
Hernando, Mississippi

Shauna Bostick
Elementary Math Specialist
Lee County School District
Tupelo, Mississippi

Samantha Brant
Teacher
Platte County School District
Platte City, Missouri

Jamie Clark
Elementary Math Coach
Allegany County Public Schools
Cumberland, Maryland

Shauna Gardner
Math and Science Instructional Coach
DeSoto County Schools
Hernando, Mississippi

Kathy Graham
Educational Consultant
Twin Falls, Idaho

Andrea Hamilton
K-5 Math Specialist
Lake Forest School District
Felton, Delaware

Susan Hankins
Instructional Coach
Tupelo Public School District
Tupelo, Mississippi

Barb Jamison
Teacher
Excelsior Springs School District
Excelsior Springs, Missouri

Pam Jones
Elementary Math Coach
Lake Region School District
Bridgton, Maine

Sherri Kane
Secondary Mathematics
Curriculum Specialist
Lee's Summit R7 School District
Lee's Summit, Missouri

Jessica Leonard
ESOL Teacher
Volusia County Schools
DeLand, Florida

Jill K. Milton
Elementary Math Coordinator
Norwood Public Schools
Norwood, Massachusetts

Jamie Pickett
Teacher
Platte County School District
Kansas City, Missouri

Mandy Schall
Math Coach
Allegany County Public Schools
Cumberland, Maryland

Marjorie Stevens
Math Consultant
Utica Community Schools
Shelby Township, Michigan

Shyree Stevenson
ELL Teacher
Penns Grove-Carneys Point
Regional School District
Penns Grove, New Jersey

Kayla Stone
Teacher
Excelsior Springs School District
Excelsior Springs, Missouri

Sara Sultan
PD Academic Trainer, Math
Tucson Unified School District
Tucson, Arizona

Angela Waltrup
Elementary Math Content Specialist
Washington County Public Schools
Hagerstown, Maryland

SAVVAS
LEARNING COMPANY

ISBN-13: 978-0-13-495467-7
ISBN-10: 0-13-495467-X
11 2023

You'll be using these digital resources throughout the year!

Digital Resources

Go to SavvasRealize.com

 Interactive Student Edition
Access online or offline.

 Interactive Additional Practice Workbook
Access online or offline.

 Math Tools
Explore math with digital tools.

 Assessment
Show what you've learned.

 Visual Learning
Interact with visual learning animations.

 Videos
Watch Math Practices Animations, Another Look Videos, and clips to support 3-Act Math.

Games
Play math games to help you learn.

 Activity
Solve a problem and share your thinking.

 Practice Buddy
Do interactive practice online.

 Glossary
A-Z Read and listen in English and Spanish.

SAVVAS
realize™ Everything you need for math anytime, anywhere

F3

Contents

Digital Resources at SavvasRealize.com

TOPICS

1. Numbers 0 to 5
2. Compare Numbers 0 to 5
3. Numbers 6 to 10
4. Compare Numbers 0 to 10
5. Classify and Count Data
6. Understand Addition
7. Understand Subtraction
8. More Addition and Subtraction
9. Count Numbers to 20
10. Compose and Decompose Numbers 11 to 19
11. Count Numbers to 100
12. Identify and Describe Shapes
13. Analyze, Compare, and Create Shapes
14. Describe and Compare Measurable Attributes

And remember your Interactive Student Edition is available at SavvasRealize.com!

SavvasRealize.com

You can count objects and write the number to tell how many in all.

11
eleven

TOPIC 9
Count Numbers to 20

enVision® STEM Project 345
Review What You Know 346
Pick a Project 347
3-ACT MATH Preview: Fresh From the Farm 348

9-1 Count, Read, and Write 11 and 12 349
K.CC.A.3, K.CC.B.5, MP.2, MP.3, MP.6

9-2 Count, Read, and Write 13, 14, and 15 353
K.CC.A.3, K.CC.B.5, MP.3, MP.6, MP.8

9-3 Count, Read, and Write 16 and 17 357
K.CC.A.3, K.CC.B.5, MP.2, MP.6, MP.7

9-4 Count, Read, and Write 18, 19, and 20 361
K.CC.A.3, K.CC.B.5, MP.5, MP.7, MP.8

9-5 Count Forward from Any Number to 20 365
K.CC.A.2, K.CC.B.4c, MP.2, MP.6, MP.7

9-6 Count to Find How Many 369
K.CC.B.5, K.CC.B.4, MP.1, MP.7, MP.8

9-7 PROBLEM SOLVING Reasoning 373
MP.2, MP.3, MP.4, K.CC.A.2, K.CC.B.5

Fluency Practice Activity 377
Vocabulary Review 378
Reteaching 379
Topic Assessment Practice 381
Topic Performance Task 383

The equation tells how many cubes in all.

$$10 + 2 = 12$$

TOPIC 10
Compose and Decompose Numbers 11 to 19

enVision® STEM Project 385

Review What You Know 386

Pick a Project 387

10-1 Make 11, 12, and 13 389
K.NBT.A.1, K.CC.B.5, MP.2, MP.4, MP.5

10-2 Make 14, 15, and 16 393
K.NBT.A.1, K.CC.B.5, MP.2, MP.3, MP.4

10-3 Make 17, 18, and 19 397
K.NBT.A.1, K.CC.B.5, MP.1, MP.2, MP.4

10-4 Find Parts of 11, 12, and 13 401
K.NBT.A.1, K.CC.B.5, MP.4, MP.6, MP.8

10-5 Find Parts of 14, 15, and 16 405
K.NBT.A.1, K.CC.B.5, MP.4, MP.5, MP.8

10-6 Find Parts of 17, 18, and 19 409
K.NBT.A.1, K.CC.B.5, MP.1, MP.4, MP.8

10-7 PROBLEM SOLVING Look For and Use Structure 413
MP.7, MP.3, MP.8, K.NBT.A.1, K.CC.B.5

Fluency Practice Activity 417

Vocabulary Review 418

Reteaching 419

Topic Assessment Practice 423

Topic Performance Task 427

SavvasRealize.com

Contents

You can use part of a hundred chart to count and find patterns.

1	2	3	4	5	6	7	8	9	10
11	12	13	14	15	16	17	18	19	20
21	22	23	24	25	26	27	28	29	30

TOPIC 11
Count Numbers to 100

enVision® STEM Project 429
Review What You Know. 430
Pick a Project 431
3-ACT MATH Preview: Stack Up 432

11-1   **Count Using Patterns to 30** 433
K.CC.A.1, K.CC.A.2, MP.2, MP.6, MP.7

11-2   **Count by Ones and by Tens to 50** 437
K.CC.A.1, K.CC.A.2, MP.1, MP.6, MP.8

11-3   **Count by Tens to 100**. 441
K.CC.A.1, K.CC.A.2, MP.3, MP.4, MP.7

11-4   **Count by Ones to 100** 445
K.CC.A.2, K.CC.A.1, MP.5, MP.7, MP.8

11-5   **PROBLEM SOLVING Look For and Use Structure** 449
MP.7, MP.6, MP.8, K.CC.A.2, K.CC.A.1

Fluency Practice Activity. 453
Vocabulary Review. 454
Reteaching 455
Topic Assessment Practice 457
Topic Performance Task 459

Contents

There are flat and solid objects in our environment. The notebook paper and envelope are flat. The cup and tissue box are solid.

TOPIC 12
Identify and Describe Shapes

enVision® STEM Project 461
Review What You Know 462
Pick a Project 463

12-1 Two-Dimensional (2-D) and Three-Dimensional (3-D) Shapes 465
K.G.A.3, K.CC.A.1, K.MD.B.3, MP.3, MP.6, MP.7

12-2 Circles and Triangles 469
K.G.A.2, K.CC.A.1, K.G.A.1, MP.2, MP.6, MP.7

12-3 Squares and Other Rectangles 473
K.G.A.2, K.CC.A.1, K.G.A.1, K.G.B.4, MP.6, MP.7, MP.8

12-4 Hexagons 477
K.G.A.2, K.CC.A.1, K.G.A.1, K.G.B.4, MP.5, MP.6, MP.7

12-5 Solid Figures 481
K.G.A.2, K.G.A.1, K.G.B.4, MP.2, MP.4, MP.7

12-6 Describe Shapes in the Environment 485
K.G.A.1, K.G.A.2, K.G.A.3, MP.1, MP.3, MP.6

12-7 PROBLEM SOLVING Precision 489
MP.6, MP.2, MP.3, K.G.A.1, K.G.A.2

Fluency Practice Activity 493
Vocabulary Review 494
Reteaching 495
Topic Assessment Practice 499
Topic Performance Task 503

SavvasRealize.com

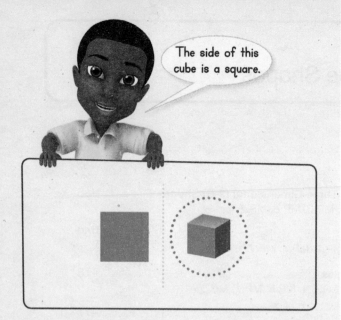

The side of this cube is a square.

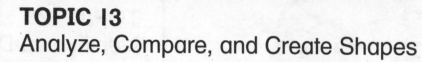

TOPIC 13
Analyze, Compare, and Create Shapes

enVision® STEM Project 505
Review What You Know. 506
Pick a Project 507
3-ACT MATH Preview: Pieced Together 508

13-1 **Analyze and Compare Two-Dimensional (2-D) Shapes** 509
K.G.B.4, K.CC.C.6, MP.4, MP.6, MP.7

13-2 **Analyze and Compare Three-Dimensional (3-D) Shapes** 513
K.G.B.4, K.CC.B.5, K.G.B.5, MP.2, MP.3, MP.7

13-3 **Compare 2-D and 3-D Shapes** 517
K.G.B.4, K.OA.A.4, MP.2, MP.5, MP.6

13-4 **PROBLEM SOLVING Make Sense and Persevere** 521
MP.1, MP.3, MP.6, K.G.B.4, K.OA.A.4, K.G.A.3

13-5 **Make 2-D Shapes from Other 2-D Shapes** 525
K.G.B.6, K.CC.B.5, K.G.A.1, K.G.B.5, MP.4, MP.7, MP.8

13-6 **Build 2-D Shapes** 529
K.G.B.5, K.CC.B.5, K.G.B.4, MP.3, MP.5, MP.7

13-7 **Build 3-D Shapes** 533
K.G.B.5, K.G.B.6, K.CC.B.5, MP.2, MP.5, MP.6

Fluency Practice Activity. 537
Vocabulary Review. 538
Reteaching 539
Topic Assessment Practice 541
Topic Performance Task 543

Contents

You can compare the sizes of different objects.

Shorter

TOPIC 14
Describe and Compare Measurable Attributes

enVision® STEM Project 545
Review What You Know. 546
Pick a Project 547

14-1   **Describe and Compare by Length and Height** 549
K.MD.A.2, K.MD.A.1, MP.2, MP.6, MP.7

14-2   **Describe and Compare by Capacity** 553
K.MD.A.2, K.MD.A.1, MP.2, MP.3, MP.8

14-3   **Describe and Compare by Weight** 557
K.MD.A.2, K.MD.A.1, MP.2, MP.3, MP.4

14-4   **Describe Objects by Measurable Attributes** 561
K.MD.A.1, MP.1, MP.2, MP.5

14-5   **Describe and Compare Objects by Measurable Attributes** 565
K.MD.A.1, K.MD.A.2, MP.2, MP.5, MP.6

14-6   **PROBLEM SOLVING Precision** 569
MP.6, MP.3, MP.5, K.MD.A.2

Fluency Practice Activity. 573
Vocabulary Review. 574
Reteaching 575
Topic Assessment Practice 577
Topic Performance Task 579

SavvasRealize.com

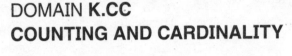

Grade K Common Core Standards

DOMAIN K.CC
COUNTING AND CARDINALITY

MAJOR CLUSTER K.OA.A
Know number names and the count sequence.

K.CC.A.1 Count to 100 by ones and by tens.

K.CC.A.2 Count forward beginning from a given number within the known sequence (instead of having to begin at 1).

K.CC.A.3 Write numbers from 0 to 20. Represent a number of objects with a written numeral 0–20 (with 0 representing a count of no objects).

MAJOR CLUSTER K.CC.B
Count to tell the number of objects.

K.CC.B.4 Understand the relationship between numbers and quantities; connect counting to cardinality.

K.CC.B.4a When counting objects, say the number names in the standard order, pairing each object with one and only one number name and each number name with one and only one object.

K.CC.B.4b Understand that the last number name said tells the number of objects counted. The number of objects is the same regardless of their arrangement or the order in which they were counted.

K.CC.B.4c Understand that each successive number name refers to a quantity that is one larger.

K.CC.B.5 Count to answer "how many?" questions about as many as 20 things arranged in a line, a rectangular array, or a circle, or as many as 10 things in a scattered configuration; given a number from 1–20, count out that many objects.

Dear Families,

The standards on the following pages describe the math that students will learn this year.

Common Core Standards

MAJOR CLUSTER K.CC.C
Compare numbers.

K.CC.C.6 Identify whether the number of objects in one group is greater than, less than, or equal to the number of objects in another group, e.g., by using matching and counting strategies.[1]

K.CC.C.7 Compare two numbers between 1 and 10 presented as written numerals.

DOMAIN K.OA
OPERATIONS AND ALGEBRAIC THINKING

MAJOR CLUSTER K.OA.A
Understand addition as putting together and adding to, and understand subtraction as taking apart and taking from.

K.OA.A.1 Represent addition and subtraction with objects, fingers, mental images, drawings[2], sounds (e.g., claps), acting out situations, verbal explanations, expressions, or equations.

K.OA.A.2 Solve addition and subtraction word problems, and add and subtract within 10, e.g., by using objects or drawings to represent the problem ([1]Students are not required to independently read the word problems.)

K.OA.A.3 Decompose numbers less than or equal to 10 into pairs in more than one way, e.g., by using objects or drawings, and record each decomposition by a drawing or equation (e.g., $5 = 2 + 3$ and $5 = 4 + 1$).

K.OA.A.4 For any number from 1 to 9, find the number that makes 10 when added to the given number, e.g., by using objects or drawings, and record the answer with a drawing or equation.

K.OA.A.5 Fluently add and subtract within 5.

DOMAIN K.NBT
NUMBER AND OPERATIONS IN BASE TEN

MAJOR CLUSTER K.NBT.A
Work with numbers 11–19 to gain foundations for place value.

K.NBT.A.1 Compose and decompose numbers from 11 to 19 into ten ones and some further ones, e.g., by using objects or drawings, and record each composition or decomposition by a drawing or equation (e.g., $18 = 10 + 8$); understand that these numbers are composed of ten ones and one, two, three, four, five, six, seven, eight, or nine ones.

DOMAIN K.MD
MEASUREMENT AND DATA

ADDITIONAL CLUSTER K.MD.A
Describe and compare measurable attributes.

K.MD.A.1 Describe measurable attributes of objects, such as length or weight. Describe several measurable attributes of a single object.

K.MD.A.2 Directly compare two objects with a measurable attribute in common, to see which object has "more of"/"less of" the attribute, and describe the difference. *For example, directly compare the heights of two children and describe one child as taller/shorter.*

SUPPORTING CLUSTER K.MD.B
Classify objects and count the number of objects in each category.

K.MD.B.3 Classify objects into given categories; count the numbers of objects in each category and sort the categories by count.[3]

Common Core Standards

DOMAIN K.G
GEOMETRY

ADDITIONAL CLUSTER K.G.A
Identify and describe shapes (squares, circles, triangles, rectangles, hexagons, cubes, cones, cylinders, and spheres).

K.G.A.1 Describe objects in the environment using names of shapes, and describe the relative positions of these objects using terms such as *above, below, beside, in front of, behind,* and *next to.*

K.G.A.2 Correctly name shapes regardless of their orientations or overall size.

K.G.A.3 Identify shapes as two-dimensional (lying in a plane, "flat") or three-dimensional ("solid").

SUPPORTING CLUSTER K.G.B
Analyze, compare, create, and compose shapes.

K.G.B.4 Analyze and compare two- and three-dimensional shapes, in different sizes and orientations, using informal language to describe their similarities, differences, parts (e.g., number of sides and vertices/"corners") and other attributes (e.g., having sides of equal length).

K.G.B.5 Model shapes in the world by building shapes from components (e.g., sticks and clay balls) and drawing shapes.

K.G.B.6 Compose simple shapes to form larger shapes. *For example, "Can you join these two triangles with full sides touching to make a rectangle?"*

---

¹Include groups with up to ten objects.
²Drawings need not show details, but should show the mathematics in the problem. (This applies wherever drawings are mentioned on the Standards.)

³Limit category counts to be less than or equal to 10.

MATHEMATICAL PRACTICES

MP.1 Make sense of problems and persevere in solving them.

MP.2 Reason abstractly and quantitatively.

MP.3 Construct viable arguments and critique the reasoning of others.

MP.4 Model with mathematics.

MP.5 Use appropriate tools strategically.

MP.6 Attend to precision.

MP.7 Look for and make use of structure.

MP.8 Look for and express regularity in repeated reasoning.

Math Practices and Problem Solving Handbook

The **Math Practices and Problem Solving Handbook** is available at SavvasRealize.com.

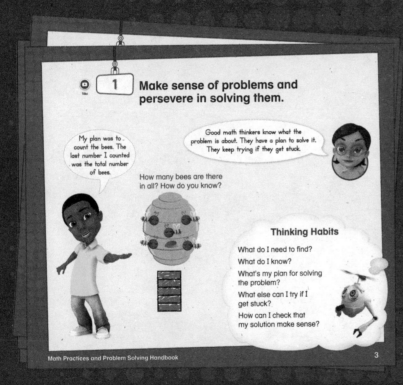

Math Practices

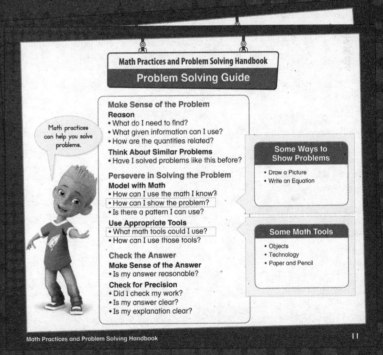

Problem Solving Guide
Problem Solving Recording Sheet

Count Numbers to 20

Essential Question: How can numbers to 20 be counted, read, written, and pictured to tell how many?

Digital Resources

Interactive Student Edition   Activity   Visual Learning   Video   Practice

Assessment   Games   Tools   Glossary

Some plants make fruit to protect their seeds.

Oranges

ënVision STEM Project: What Can We Get From Plants?

Directions Read the character speech bubbles to students. **Find Out!** Have students find out ways plants impact and change their environment. Say: *Talk to friends and relatives about what plants do for the environment. Ask them how humans and animals use things in the environment, such as plants, to meet their needs.* **Journal: Make a Poster** Have students make a poster. Ask them to draw some ways that plants can provide food and shelter for animals and humans. Finally, have students draw an orange tree with 15 oranges.

Name _____

Review What You Know

1

$$5 + 4 = 9$$

$$5 - 4 = 1$$

2

$$6 - 3 = 3$$

3

$$7 - 4 = 3$$

4

 5   15   10

5

_____   _____   _____

------- + ------- = -------

_____   _____   _____

Directions Have students: **1** draw a circle around the equation that shows addition; **2** draw a circle around the minus sign; **3** draw a circle around the difference; **4** draw a circle around the correct number of counters shown; **5** count the red counters, count the yellow counters, and then write the equation to find the sum.

Name _____

A

B

C

Directions Say: *You will choose one of these projects. Look at picture* **A.** *Think about this question: Can you count all these gum balls? If you choose Project A, you will play a counting game to 20. Look at picture* **B.** *Think about this question: What is your favorite sport? If you choose Project B, you will tell a sports story using numbers. Look a picture* **C.** *Think about this question: What kinds of fish make good pets? If you choose this project, you will make a model of a fish tank.*

3-ACT MATH PREVIEW

Math Modeling

Fresh From the Farm

Video

Uh-oh! How did that happen?

Directions Read the robot's speech bubble to students. **Generate Interest** Ask students what vegetables they enjoy most. Say: *What vegetables might be used to make a salad? What vegetable do you like?* Have your class decide which vegetables they would buy for a salad.

I can ...
model with math to count groups and compare to solve a problem.

Ⓒ Mathematical Practices MP.4
Also MP.6, MP.7
Content Standards K.CC.B.5
Also K.CC.A.2, K.CC.A.3, K.OA.A.2

348 three hundred forty-eight

Topic 9 | 3-Act Math

Solve & Share

Name _____

Activity

Directions Say: *Carlos has a collection of toy cars. How can Carlos show the number of cars he has? Use counters and put them together in two different ways so they can be counted easily. Draw your counters to show one of your ways.*

I can ...
count and write the numbers 11 and 12.

Content Standards K.CC.A.3
Also K.CC.B.5
Mathematical Practices MP.2, MP.3, and MP.6

eleven

☆ **Guided Practice**

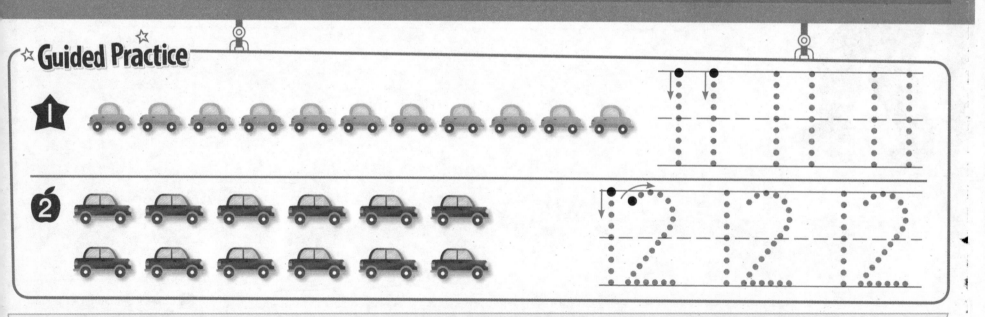

1

2

Directions 🌟 and ② Have students count the cars in each group, and then practice writing the number that tells how many.

Name _____

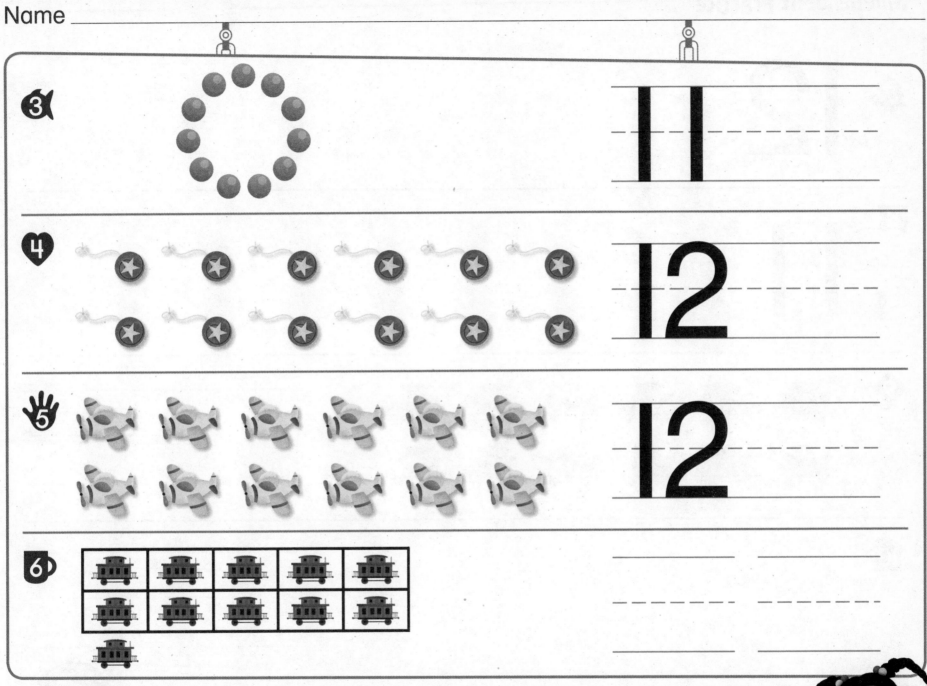

❸ 11

♥ 12

✋ 12

☕ _____ _____

Directions ❸–✋ Have students count the toys in each group, use counters to show how many, and then practice writing the number that tells how many. ☕ **Number Sense** Have students count the train cars, write the number to tell how many, and then write the number that comes after it.

Topic 9 | Lesson 1   three hundred fifty-one 351

Independent Practice

 **7** 12

8 11

9

_____

- - - - - - - - - - -

_____

10

_____

- - - - - - - - - - -

_____

Directions 7–8 Have students use counters to make the number and draw circles to show how many. **9** Have students count the toys, and then practice writing the number that tells how many. **10 Higher Order Thinking** Have students draw 11 toys, and then practice writing the number that tells how many.

352 three hundred fifty-two

Topic 9 | Lesson 1

Solve & Share

Name _____

Activity

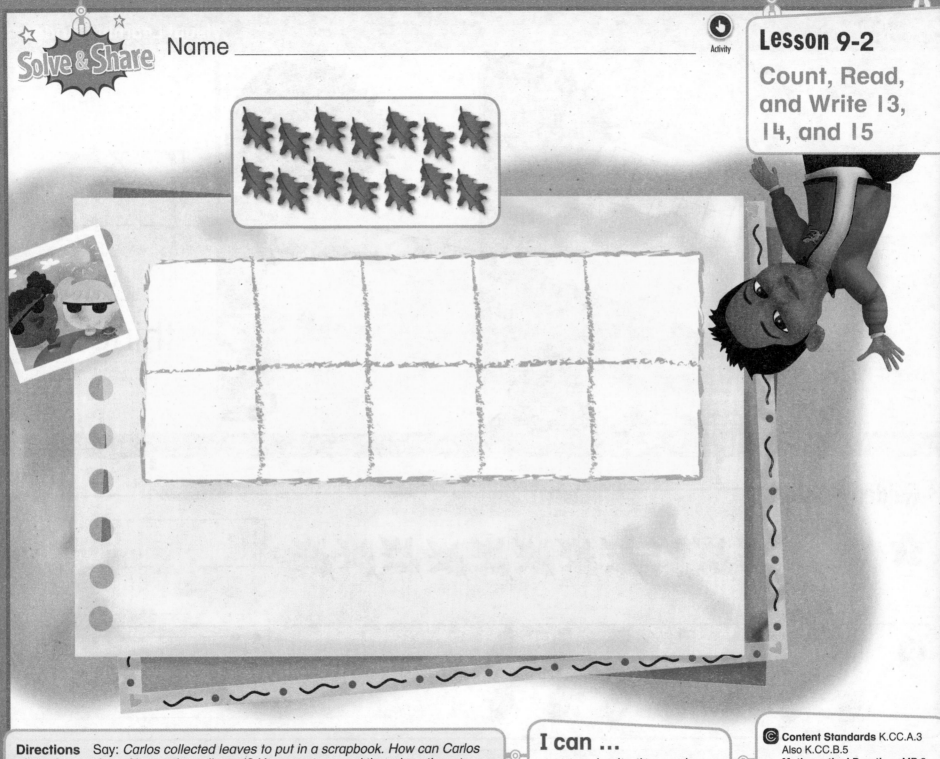

Directions Say: *Carlos collected leaves to put in a scrapbook. How can Carlos show the number of leaves he collected? Use counters, and then draw them to show one way.*

I can ...
count and write the numbers 13, 14, and 15.

© **Content Standards** K.CC.A.3 Also K.CC.B.5
Mathematical Practices MP.3, MP.6, and MP.8

13

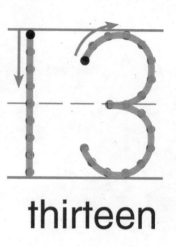

thirteen

☆ **Guided Practice**

1

2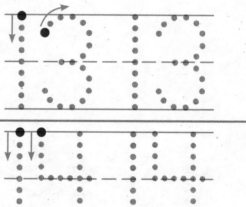

Directions 🟊 and ❷ Have students count the leaves in each group, and then practice writing the number that tells how many.

Name _____

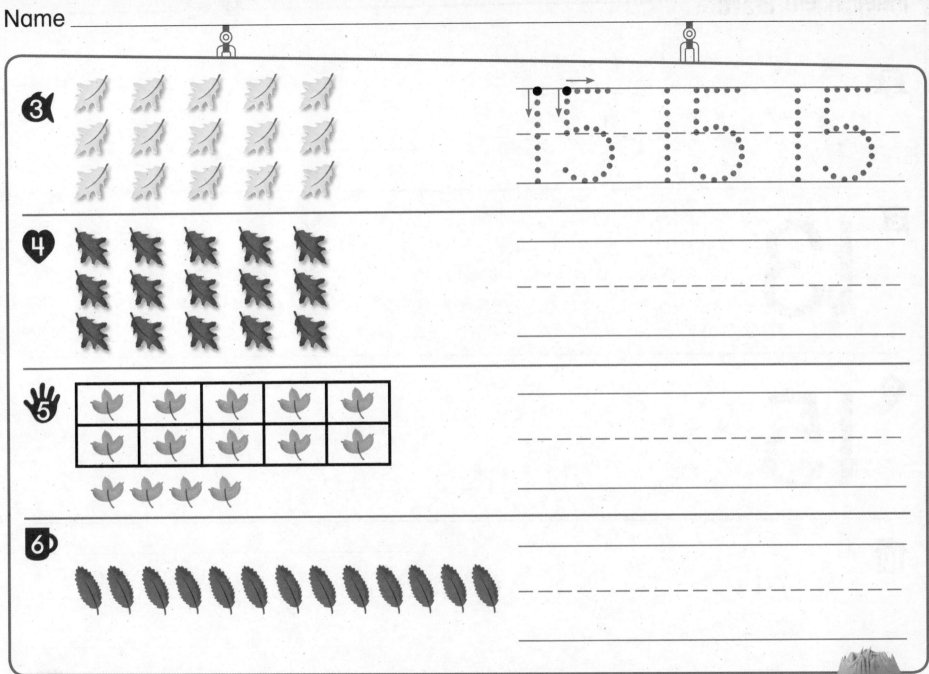

3   15 15 15 15

4

5

6

Directions ❸–❹ Have students count the leaves in each group, use counters to show how many, and then practice writing the number that tells how many. ✋ Have students count the leaves, and then practice writing the number that tells how many. ☕ **enVision® STEM** Say: *Trees use their leaves to turn sunlight into food.* Have students count the green leaves, and then practice writing the number that tells how many.

Independent Practice

7

---

8 13

---

9 15

10

Topic 9 | Lesson 2

Name _____

Activity

Lesson 9-3
Count, Read, and Write 16 and 17

Directions Say: *Jada has a collection of piggy banks. She displays her piggy banks in 2 rows, as shown on the page. Count the piggy banks and use red cubes to show how many in all. Then use blue cubes to show another way to display the same number of piggy banks. Draw the cubes to show your answer.*

I can ...
count and write the numbers 16 and 17.

© **Content Standards** K.CC.A.3 Also K.CC.B.5
Mathematical Practices MP.2, MP.6, and MP.7

Visual Learning · A-Z Glossary

17

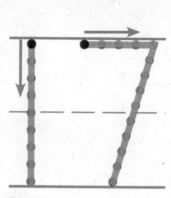

seventeen

☆ Guided Practice

1

2

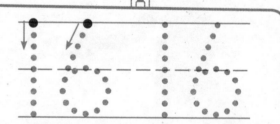

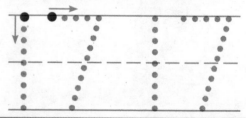

Directions 1 and 2 Have students count the piggy banks in each group, use cubes to show how many, and then practice writing the number that tells how many.

Name _____

3 _____

4 _____

5 _____

Directions **3**–**5** Have students count the stuffed animals in each group, use cubes to show how many, and then practice writing the number that tells how many.

Topic 9 | Lesson 3

three hundred fifty-nine **359**

Independent Practice

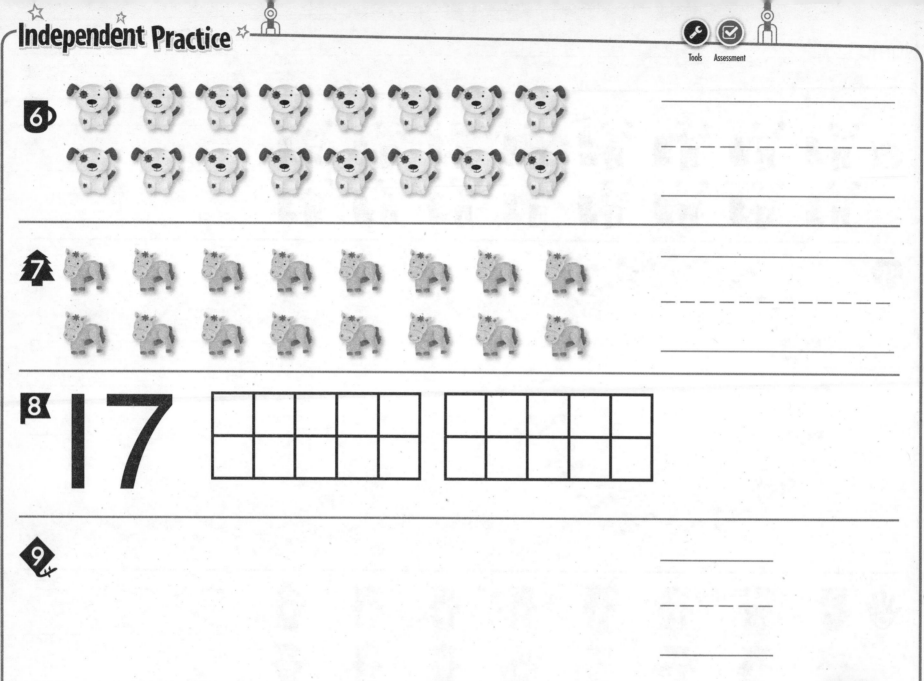

6 _____

7 _____

8 17

9 _____

Directions **6–7** Have students count the stuffed animals in each group, and then practice writing the number that tells how many. **8** Have students use counters to make the number and use ten-frames or draw circles to show how many. **⋄ Higher Order Thinking** Have students draw 17 balls, and then practice writing the number that tells how many.

Topic 9 | Lesson 3

Name _____

Directions Say: *Carlos has a collection of bird stickers in his sticker album. How can Carlos show the number of bird stickers he has? Use counters, and then draw them to show one way.*

I can ...
count and write the numbers 18, 19, and 20.

© **Content Standards** K.CC.A.3 Also K.CC.B.5
Mathematical Practices MP.5, MP.7, and MP.8

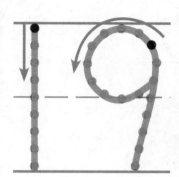

19

nineteen

☆ Guided Practice

 1

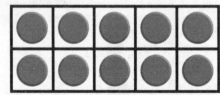 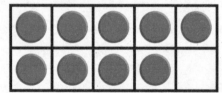 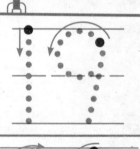

2

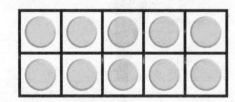 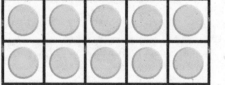   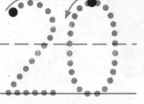

Directions ★ and ❷ Have students count the counters showing how many red and blue bird stickers Carlos has in his collection, and then practice writing the number.

 Topic 9 | Lesson 4

Name _____

3

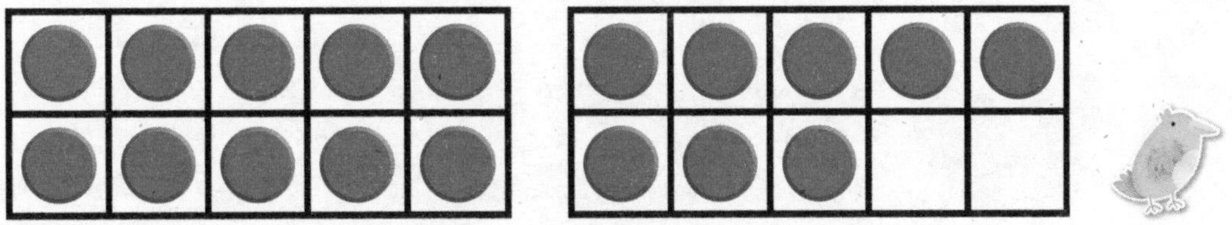

4

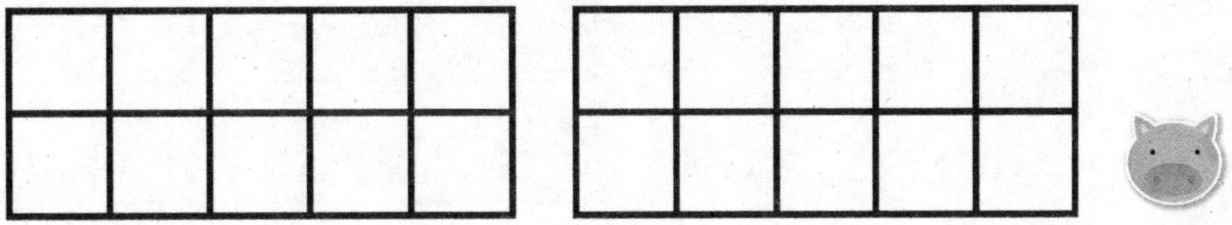

19

5

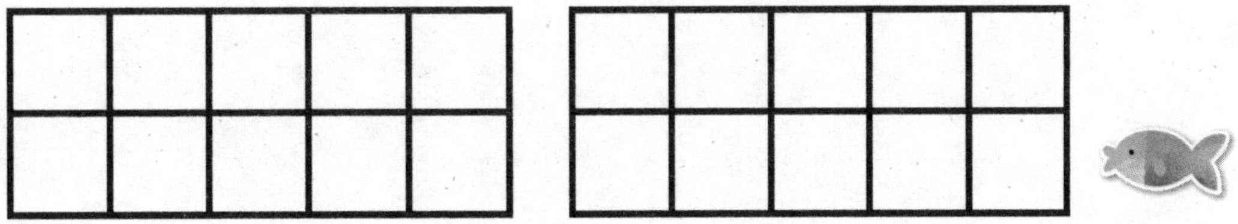

20

6

_____

- - - - - - - - - - - - - - - -

_____

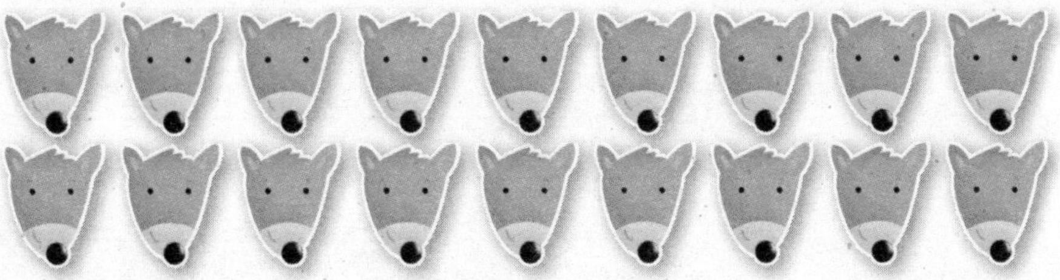

Directions **3** Have students count the counters showing how many yellow bird stickers Carlos has in his collection, and then practice writing the number. **4**–**5** Have students use counters to make each number and draw counters in the ten-frames to show how many. **6** Have students count the stickers, and then practice writing the number that tells how many.

Independent Practice

7

- - - - - - - - - - - - - - - - - -

8

- - - - - - - - - - - - - - - - - -

9 19

10

- - - - - - - - - - - - - - - - - -

Directions **7** and **8** Have students count the stickers in each group, and then practice writing the number that tells how many. **9** Have students use counters to make the number and draw circles to show how many. **10** **Higher Order Thinking** Have students draw 20 bug stickers, and then practice writing the number that tells how many.

364 three hundred sixty-four   **Topic 9** | **Lesson 4**

Name _____

Activity

Start

2

End

Directions Say: *Put 12 counters on the double ten-frame. Write the number to tell how many. Put 1 more counter on the double ten-frame, and then write the number. Repeat using 1 more counter. What do you notice about the numbers? Do they get larger or smaller as you count?*

I can ...
count forward from any number to a number within 20.

© **Content Standards** K.CC.A.2 Also K.CC.B.4c
Mathematical Practices MP.2, MP.6, and MP.7

1	2	3	4	5	6	7	8	9	10
11	12	13	14	15	16	17	18	19	20

Count forward.

8 9 10 11 12 13

☆ Guided Practice

1	2	3	4	5	6	7	8	9	10
11	12	13	14	15	16	17	18	19	20

15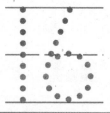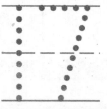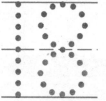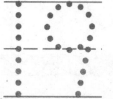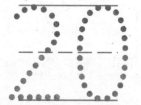

Directions ★ Have students find the blue number on the number chart, count forward until they reach the stop sign, and then write each number they counted.

366 three hundred sixty-six

Topic 9 | Lesson 5

Name _____

2 🍎

1	2	3	4	5	6	7	(8)	9	10
11	12	13	14	15	16	17	18	19	20

3

3 🐟

1	2	3	4	5	6	7	8	9	10
11	12	13	14	15	(16)	17	18	19	20

11

4 ♥

1	2	3	4	5	6	7	8	9	10
11	12	13	14	15	16	17	(18)	19	20

13

Directions **2–4** Have students find the blue number on the number chart, count forward until they reach the stop sign, and then write each number they counted.

three hundred sixty-seven **367**

Independent Practice

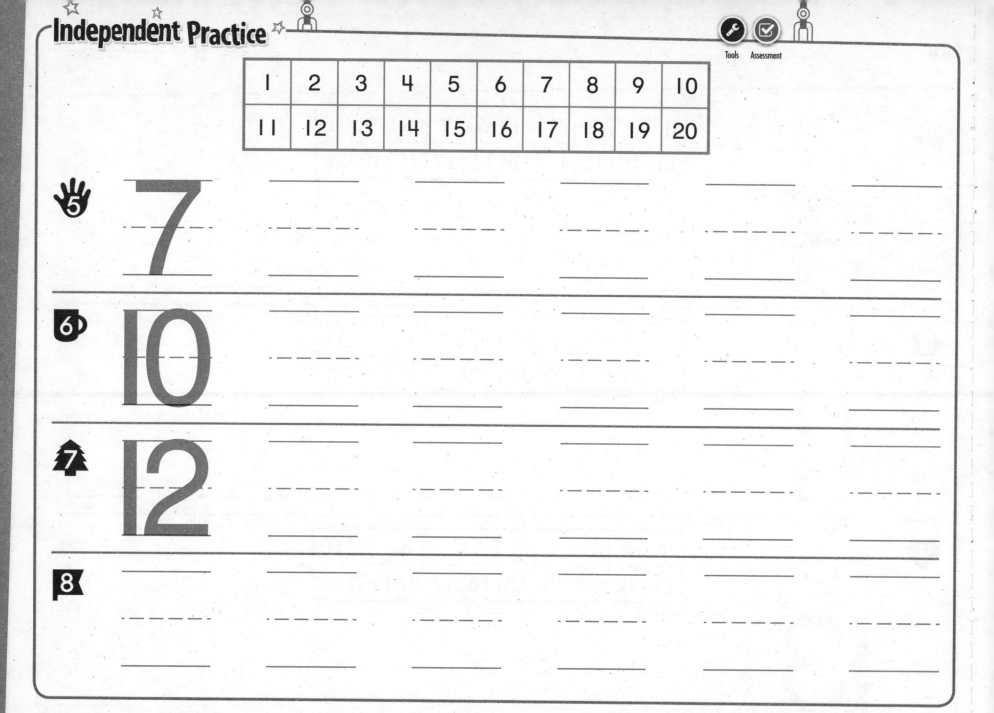

1	2	3	4	5	6	7	8	9	10
11	12	13	14	15	16	17	18	19	20

Tools   Assessment

7

10

12

8

Directions Say: *Daniel has 13 cherries on a tray. Jada has 11 cherries on a tray. How can you show this? Use counters to show the cherries on the trays, and then draw the pictures. How can you tell that your drawings are correct?*

I can ...
count to find how many are in a group.

 Content Standards K.CC.B.5
Also K.CC.B.4
Mathematical Practices MP.1,
MP.7, and MP.8

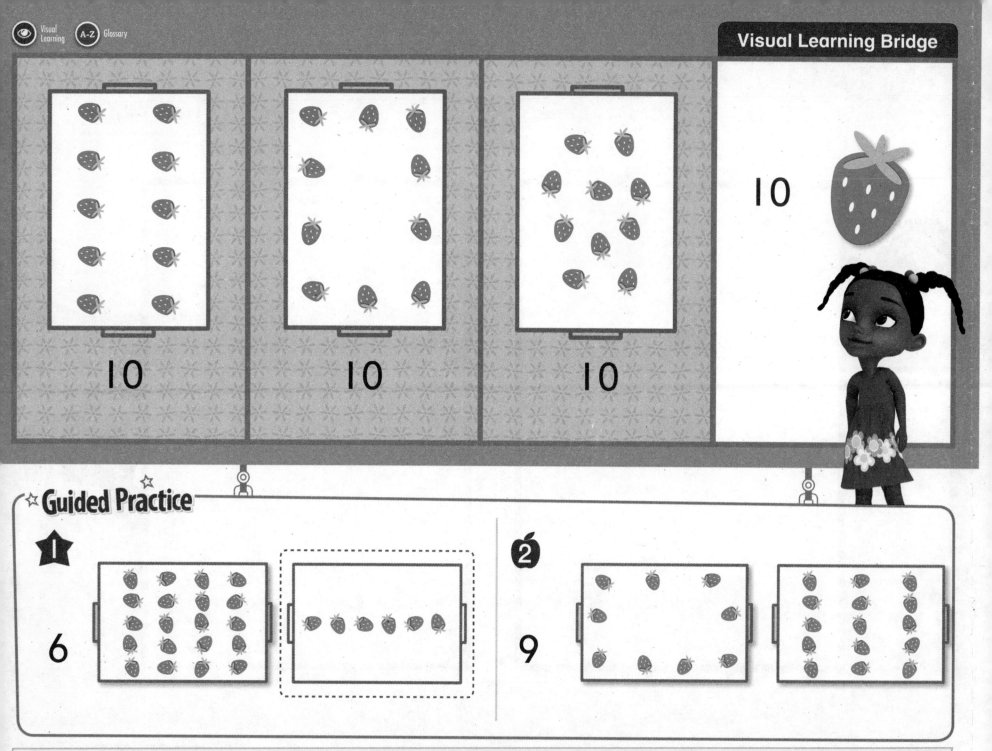

10   10   10   10

☆ Guided Practice

1 6

2 9

Directions Have students count to find how many. Then: ⭐ draw a circle around the tray with 6 strawberries; 🍎 draw a circle around the tray with 9 strawberries.

Name

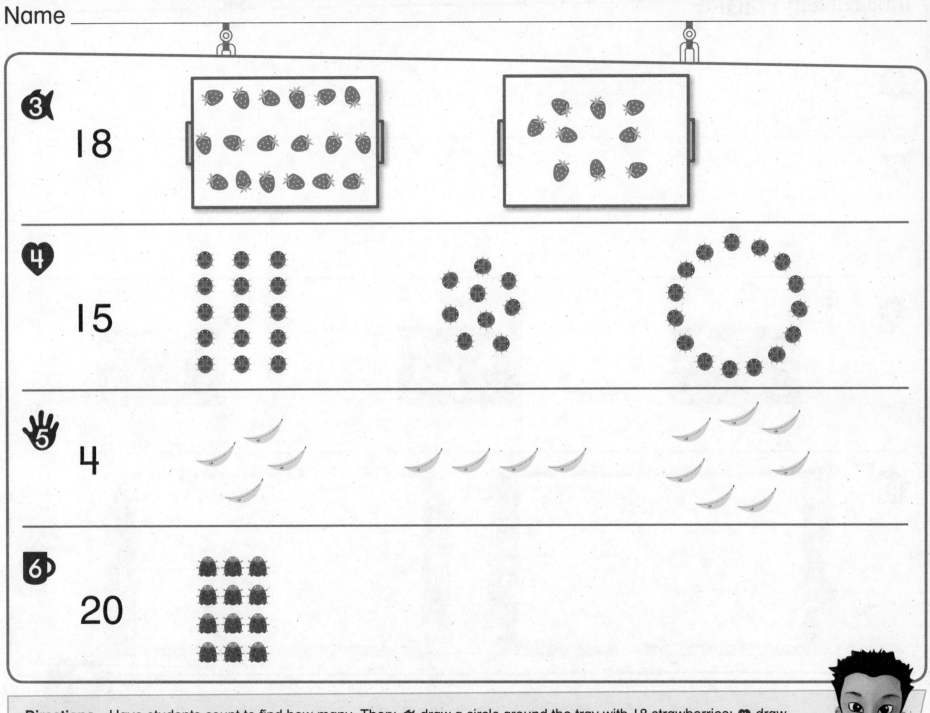

3️⃣ 18

4️⃣ 15

5️⃣ 4

6️⃣ 20

Directions Have students count to find how many. Then: 3️⃣ draw a circle around the tray with 18 strawberries; 4️⃣ draw a circle around the groups with 15 bugs; 5️⃣ draw a circle around the groups with 4 bananas. 6️⃣ **Algebra** Have students count the bugs in the group, and then draw another group of bugs so that there are 20 bugs in all.

Independent Practice

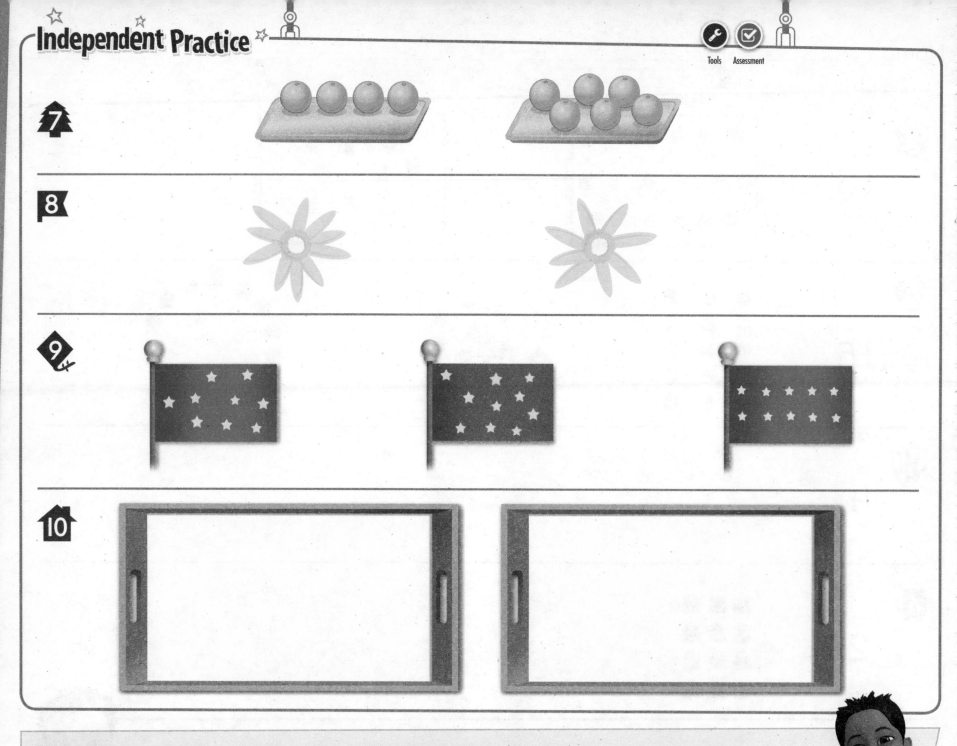

7

8

9

10

Directions Have students count to find how many. Then: **7** draw a circle around the tray with 6 oranges; **8** draw a circle around the flower with 8 petals; **9** draw a circle around the flags with 10 stars. **10** **Higher Order Thinking** Have students draw 19 strawberries in two different ways.

     Topic 9 | **Lesson 6**

10   11   12   13   14

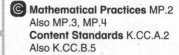

Directions Say: *Carlos wants to put some or all of the eggs in the carton. Draw a circle around all the numbers that tell how many eggs he could put in the carton. Explain why there could be more than one answer.*

I can ...

use reasoning to count and write numbers to the number 20.

© **Mathematical Practices** MP.2
Also MP.3, MP.4
Content Standards K.CC.A.2
Also K.CC.B.5

Think. 10, 11, 12, 13, or 14?

I see 12.

3 possible answers

Guided Practice

1

8   9   (10)   (11)   (12)

Directions Say: *There are more than 8 cows on a farm. Some cows are outside the barn. 1 or more cows are inside the barn. Count the cows that are outside of the barn, and then draw a circle around the numbers that tell how many cows there could be in all.*

Topic 9 | Lesson 7

Name _____

☆ ☆ ☆
Independent Practice ☆

Tools   Assessment

2

12   13   14   15   16

3

16   17   18   19   20

4

3   4   5   6   7

Directions Say: **2** *There is 1 more than 12 horses outside the stable. 0, 1, or 2 horses are inside the stable. Draw a circle around the number of horses outside the stable, and then draw a circle around the numbers that tell how many horses there could be in all.* **3** *There is 1 more than 16 dogs playing in the park. 1 or 2 dogs are resting in a doghouse. Draw a circle around the numbers that tell how many dogs there could be in all.* **4** *The fish tank can hold up to 15 fish. Count the fish in the tank, and then draw a circle around the numbers that tell how many more fish could fit in the tank.*

Topic 9 | Lesson 7

three hundred seventy-five   **375**

Problem Solving

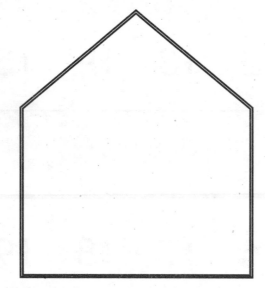

10 11 12 13 14

Directions Read the problem to students. Then have them use multiple problem-solving methods to solve the problem. Say: *Alex lives on a farm with so many cats that they are hard to count. Sometimes the cats are outside and sometimes they hide in the shed. Alex knows that the number of cats is greater than 11. There are less than 15 cats on the farm. How can Alex find out the number of cats that could be on his farm?* ✋ **Reasoning** *What numbers do you know from the problem? Mark an X on the numbers that do NOT fit the clues. Draw a circle around the numbers that tell the number of cats that could be on the farm.* ➏ **Model** *How can you show a word problem using pictures? Draw a picture of the cats on Alex's farm. Remember that some may hide inside the shed.* ➐ **Explain** *Is your drawing complete? Tell a friend how your drawing shows the number of cats on Alex's farm.*

Show the Letter   Name _____

⭐1

2 + 3	5 − 1	2 + 2	1 + 3	4 − 0
5 − 2	0 + 4	0 + 3	2 + 1	1 + 4
2 − 1	3 + 1	5 − 1	4 + 0	1 + 3
3 + 0	2 + 2	5 − 3	5 − 4	2 + 0
1 − 1	4 − 0	2 − 0	3 + 2	1 + 0

②

_____

— — — — —

_____

I can ...
add and subtract fluently to 5.

© **Content Standard** K.OA.A.5
Mathematical Practices MP.3, MP.6, MP.7, and MP.8

Directions Have students: ⭐ color each box that has a sum or difference that is equal to 4; ② write the letter they see.

 A-Z Glossary

1 ⭐

13   16   18

2 🍎

12   15   17

3

_____

- - - - - - - - - - -

_____

4 ❤️

[box]

- - - - - - - - - - -

_____

5 ✋

6 ☕

_____

- - - - - - - - - - -

_____

Directions **Understand Vocabulary** Have students: ⭐ draw a circle around the number **sixteen**; 🍎 draw a circle around the number **twelve**; **3** write the number **eighteen**; ❤️ draw **eleven** counters in the box, and then write the number; ✋ draw a circle around **fourteen** cubes; ☕ write the number **twenty**.

Name _____

Set A

19

☆1

②

Set B

③

1	2	3	4	5	6	7	8	9	10
11	12	13	14	15	⑯	17	18	19	20

1	2	3	4	5	6	7	8	9	10
⑪	12	13	14	15	16	17	18	19	20

14 15 16

9

Directions Have students: ☆ and ② count the objects in each group, and then write the number to tell how many; ③ find the blue number on the number chart, count forward until they reach the stop sign, and then write each number they counted.

Set C

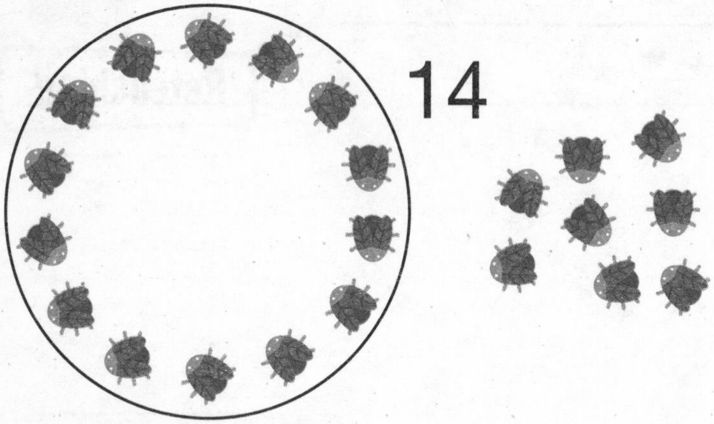

14

4

15

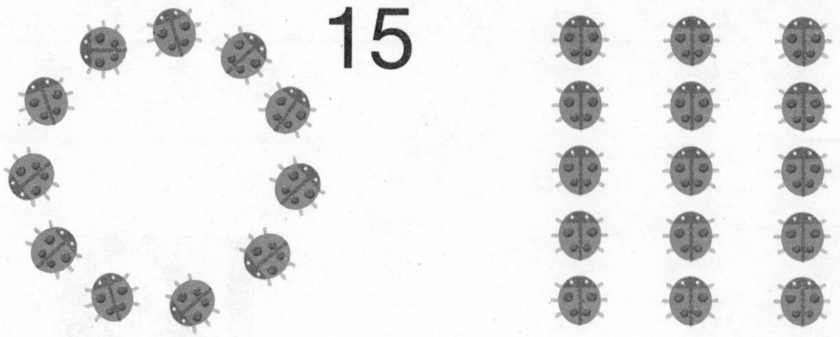

Set D

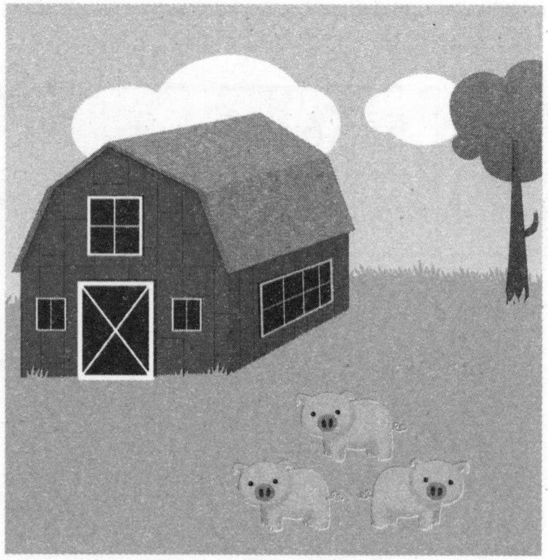

2 3 4 5

5

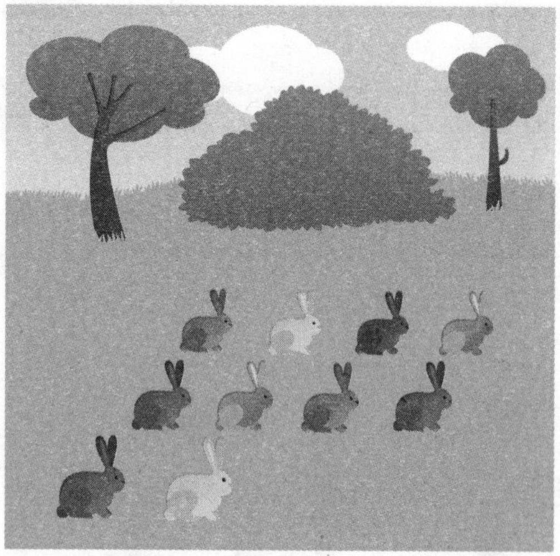

9 10 11 12 13

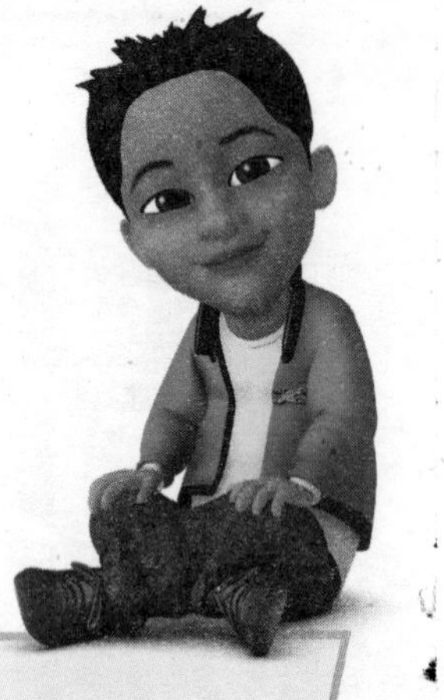

Directions Have students: 4 draw a circle around the group with 15 bugs; 5 listen to the story and use reasoning to find the answer. *Some bunnies are resting in the grass. 2 or 3 bunnies are playing behind the bush. Count the bunnies in the grass, and then draw a circle around the numbers that show how many bunnies there could be in all.*

Name _____

 1
(A) 13

(B) 14

(C) 15

(D) 16

2
(A)

(B)

(C)

(D)

3

14 □   15 □   16 □   17 □   12 □

Directions Have students mark the best answer. **1** Which number tells how many? **2** Which shows 11? **3** Have students listen to the story, and then mark all the possible answers. *There are some bees outside of the beehive. 1 or more bees are inside the beehive. Count the bees outside of the beehive, and then mark three numbers that tell how many bees there could be in all.*

4

_____

- - - - -

_____

5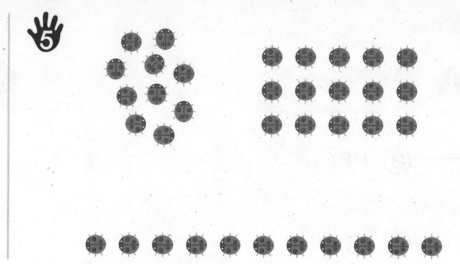

6

_____

- - - - -

_____

7

1	2	3	4	5	6	7	8	9	10
11	12	13	14	15	16	17	(18)	19	20

_____   _____

- - - - -   - - - - -

_____

Directions Have students: **4** count the leaves, and then write the number to tell how many; **5** draw a circle around the group that shows 15 ladybugs; **6** draw eighteen marbles, and then write the number to tell how many; **7** find the blue number on the number chart, count forward until they reach the stop sign, and then write each number they counted.

 Topic 9 | Assessment Practice

Name _____

⭐ 1

♥ _____
  - - - - -
  _____

🍎 2

😊 _____
  - - - - -
  _____

Directions **Sadie's Stickers** Say: *Sadie puts many stickers in her notebook. How many of each type of sticker is there?* Have students:
⭐ count the number of heart stickers, and then write the number to tell how many; 2 count the number of smiley face stickers, and then write the number to tell how many.

3

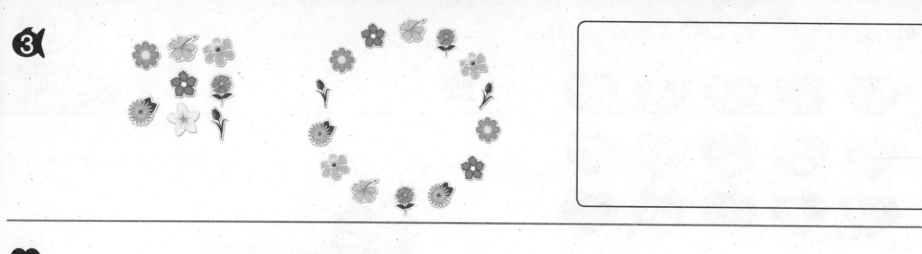

4

10 _____ _____

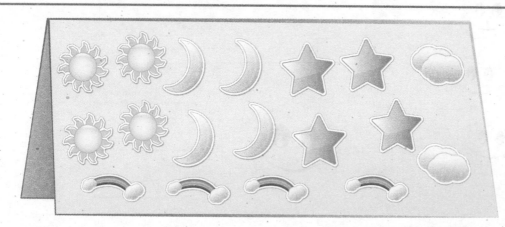**5**

16   17   18   19   20

Directions **3** Say: *Sadie wants to use 14 stickers to decorate a picture frame.* Have students draw a circle around the group of stickers that she should use, and then draw a different way to show 14 stickers. **4** Say: *Sadie gets a sticker for feeding her dog every day. She has fed her dog for 10 days. How many stickers will Sadie have in 2 more days?* Have students count forward by 2 more days to find the answer, and then write each number they counted. **5** Say: *Sadie puts 18 stickers on the front of a card. She puts 1 or more stickers on the back of a card.* Have students draw a circle around the numbers that show how many stickers there could be in all. Have students explain their answer.

Topic 9 | Performance Task

Compose and Decompose Numbers 11 to 19

Essential Question: How can composing and decomposing numbers from 11 to 19 into ten ones and some further ones help you understand place value?

Digital Resources

Interactive Student Edition · Activity · Visual Learning · Video · Practice

Assessment · Games · Tools · Glossary

A desert

Sunlight causes water to evaporate faster.

ēnVision STEM Project: Sunlight and Earth's Surface

Directions Read the character speech bubbles to students. **Find Out!** Have students find out how sunlight affects Earth's surface. Say: *Talk to friends and relatives about sunlight and how it affects Earth.* **Journal: Make a Poster** Have students make a poster that shows 3 things sunlight does for Earth. Have them draw a sun with 16 rays. Then have them write an equation for parts of 16.

Name _____

Review What You Know

★1 (fish groups)

❷2 (fish groups)

◀3 (fish groups)

♥4 (leaves in a row)

_____

- - - - - - - - - - - - -

✋5 (leaves in a circle)

_____

- - - - - - - - - - - - -

☕6 (leaves in rows)

_____

- - - - - - - - - - - - -

Directions Have students: **★** draw a circle around the group with 16; **❷** draw a circle around the group with 20; **◀** draw a circle around the group that is less than the other group; **♥–☕** count the leaves, and then write the number to tell how many.

Name _____

A

B

Directions Say: *You will choose one of these projects. Look at picture A. Think about this question: How great is the great outdoors? If you choose Project A, you will tell a camping story. Look at picture B. Think about this question: What do mice like to eat? If you choose Project B, you will make a mouse poster.*

C

D

Directions Say: *You will choose one of these projects. Look at picture* **C.** *Think about this question: What do you like to collect? If you choose Project C, you will make a sticker book. Look at picture* **D.** *Think about this question: What is in a granola bar? If you choose Project D, you will make a snack-time drawing.*

Topic 10 | Pick a Project

Solve & Share

Name _____

$$10 + \underline{\quad\quad} = \underline{\quad\quad}$$

I can ...
use drawings and equations to make the numbers 11, 12, and 13.

© **Content Standards** K.NBT.A.1 Also K.CC.B.5
Mathematical Practices MP.2, MP.4, and MP.5

Directions Say: *Use counters to fill the ten-frame. Put 1, 2, or 3 counters outside of the ten-frame. Draw all of the counters. What equation can you write to tell how many counters there are in all?*

 Go Online | SavvasRealize.com

How many?

10 + 3 = 13

13

☆ Guided Practice

1

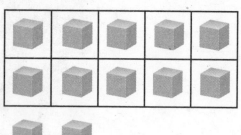

$$10 + 2 = 12$$

Directions ⭐ Have students write an equation to match the number of blocks shown. Then have them tell how the picture and equation show 10 ones and some more ones.

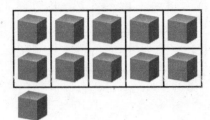

_____ _____ _____

- - - - - + - - - - - = - - - - -

_____ _____ _____

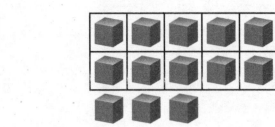

_____ _____ _____

- - - - - + - - - - - = - - - - -

_____ _____ _____

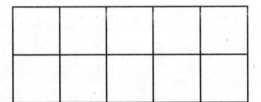 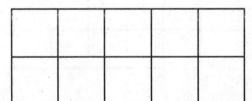

10 + 2 = 12   10 + 3 = 13

Directions Have students: ❷ and ❸ write an equation to match the number of blocks shown. Then have them tell how the picture and equation show 10 ones and some more ones; ❹ and ✋ draw blocks to match the equation. Then have them tell how the picture and equation show 10 ones and some more ones.

_____ _____ _____

- - - - - + - - - - - = - - - - -

_____

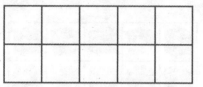

_____ _____ _____

- - - - - + - - - - - = - - - - -

_____

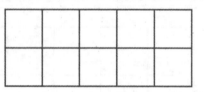

_____

10 + - - - - - = 12

_____

13 = 10 + - - - - -

_____

Directions Have students: 6 draw counters and write an equation to show how to make 13. Then have them tell how the picture and equation show 10 ones and some more ones; 7 draw counters and write an equation to show how to make 11. Then have them tell how the picture and equation show 10 ones and some more ones. 8 **Algebra** Have students draw counters to find the missing number. Then have them tell how the picture and equation show 10 ones and some more ones. 9 **Higher Order Thinking** Have students draw counters to find the missing number. Then have them tell how the picture and equation show 10 ones and some more ones.

Topic 10 | Lesson 1

$$ \underline{} + \underline{} = 15 $$

Directions Say: *Put 15 counters in the double ten-frame to show 10 ones and some more ones. Then complete the equation to match the counters.*

I can ...
make the numbers 14, 15, and 16.

© **Content Standards** K.NBT.A.1
Also K.CC.B.5
Mathematical Practices MP.2, MP.3, and MP.4

Topic 10 | Lesson 2

Go Online | SavvasRealize.com

three hundred ninety-three **393**

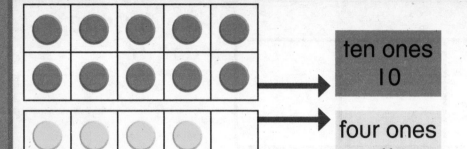

ten ones
10

four ones
4

14 counters

$$10 + 4 = 14$$

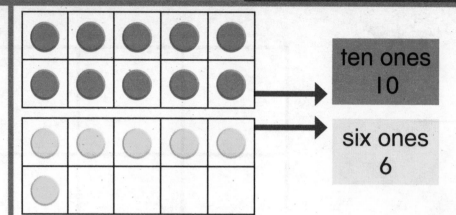

ten ones
10

six ones
6

16 counters

$$10 + 6 = 16$$

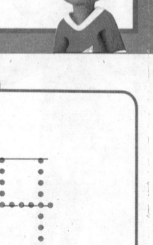

☆ Guided Practice

 ⭐ 1

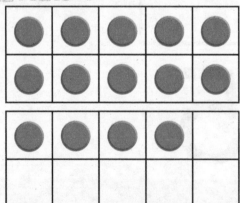

$$10 + 4 = 14$$

Directions ⭐ Have students write an equation to match the counters. Then have them tell how the picture and equation show 10 ones and some more ones.

Topic 10 | Lesson 2

2

(ten-frame with 10 counters)

(ten-frame with 5 counters)

_____ _____

- - - - - + - - - - - = - - - - -

3

(ten-frame with 10 counters)

(ten-frame with 6 counters)

_____ _____

- - - - - + - - - - - = - - - - -

4

(two ten-frames)

$$10 + 4 = 14$$

5

(two ten-frames)

$$10 + 5 = 15$$

Directions Have students: **2**–**3** write an equation to match the counters. Then have them tell how the picture and equation show 10 ones and some more ones; **4**–**5** draw counters to match the equation. Then have them tell how the picture and equation show 10 ones and some more ones.

Independent Practice

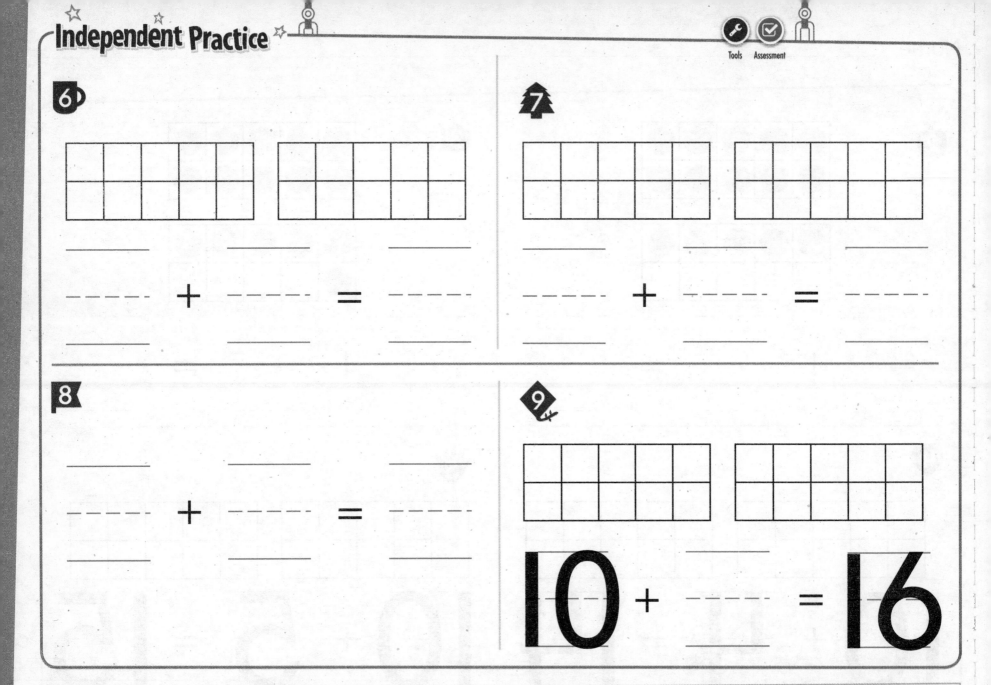

6

_____ _____

_ _ _ _ _ **+** _ _ _ _ _ **=** _ _ _ _ _

_____ _____

7

_____ _____

_ _ _ _ _ **+** _ _ _ _ _ **=** _ _ _ _ _

_____ _____

8

_____ _____

_ _ _ _ _ **+** _ _ _ _ _ **=** _ _ _ _ _

_____

9

10 + _ _ _ _ _ = 16

Directions Have students: **6** draw counters and write an equation to show how to make 16. Then have them tell how the picture and equation show 10 ones and some more ones; **7** draw counters and write an equation to show how to make 14. Then have them tell how the picture and equation show 10 ones and some more ones. **8 Number Sense** Have students write an equation to show 15 as 10 ones and some more ones. **9 Higher Order Thinking** Have students draw counters to find the missing number in the equation. Then have them tell how the picture and equation show 10 ones and some more ones.

396 three hundred ninety-six

Topic 10 | Lesson 2

Solve & Share

_____   _ _ _ _   _ _ _ _

\- \- \- \- \-   +   \- \- \- \-   =   \- \- \- \- \-

Directions Say: *Jada made 10 prizes for the school carnival. She makes 8 more. Use counters to show how many prizes Jada made in all. Then write an equation to match the counters, and tell how the counters and equation show 10 ones and some more ones.*

I can ... make the numbers 17, 18, and 19.

© **Content Standards** K.NBT.A.1 Also K.CC.B.5 **Mathematical Practices** MP.1, MP.2, and MP.4

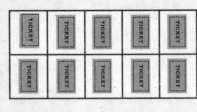

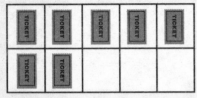

$$10 + 7 = 17$$

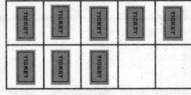

$$10 + 8 = 18$$

$$10 + 9 = 19$$

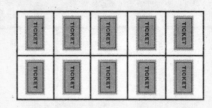

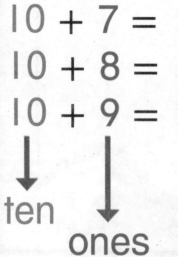

$$10 + 7 = 17$$
$$10 + 8 = 18$$
$$10 + 9 = 19$$

ten   ones   sum

 Guided Practice

1

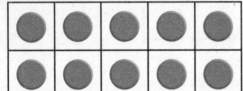

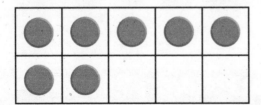

$$10 + 7 = 17$$

Directions ⭐ Have students complete the equation to match the counters. Then have them tell how the picture and equation show 10 ones and some more ones.

Topic 10 | Lesson 3

Name _____

2

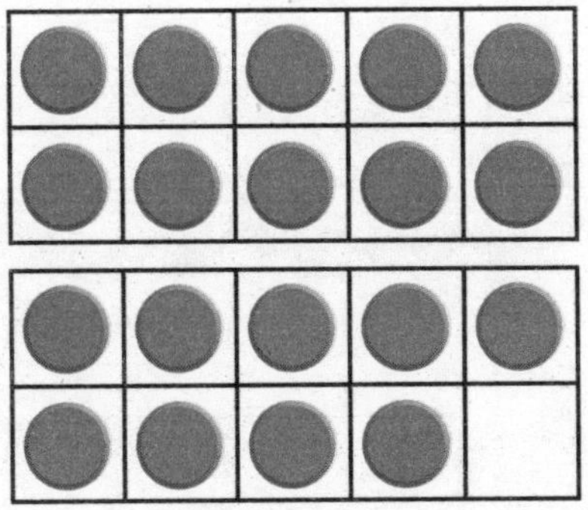

\- - - - - -   +   - - - - - -   =   - - - - - -

_____

3

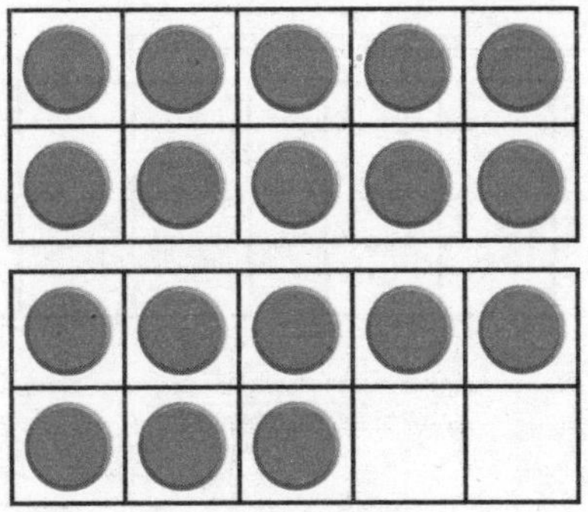

\- - - - - -   +   - - - - - -   =   - - - - - -

_____

4

_____

10 + - - - - - = - - - - -

5

_____

10 + - - - - - = - - - - -

Directions Have students: **2** and **3** write an equation to match the counters. Then have them tell how the picture and equation show 10 ones and some more ones; **4** and **5** complete the equation to match the cubes. Then have them tell how the picture and equation show 10 ones and some more ones.

Tools Assessment

6 ____ + ____ = ____

7 ____ + ____ = ____

8 ____ + ____ = ____

9 10 + ____ = 19

Solve & Share

Name _____

Activity

Lesson 10-4
Find Parts of
11, 12, and 13

13 = _____ + _____

_____

Directions Say: *13 students wait for the train. There are only 10 seats in each train car. How many students will have to ride in a second car? Use counters to show your work. Then tell how the counters and equation show 10 ones and some more ones.*

I can ...
find parts of the numbers 11, 12, and 13 when one part is 10.

© **Content Standards** K.NBT.A.1 Also K.CC.B.5 **Mathematical Practices** MP.4, MP.6, and MP.8

Topic 10 | Lesson 4

 Go Online | SavvasRealize.com

four hundred one **401**

13 wins!

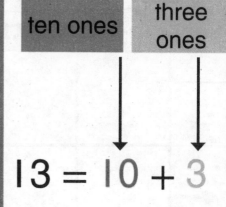

ten ones	three ones

$$13 = 10 + 3$$

ten ones
10

three ones
3

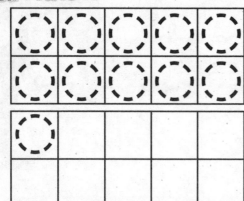

☆ **Guided Practice**

$$11 = 10 + 1$$

Directions 🌟 Have students use counters to show 11, draw them in the double ten-frame, and complete the equation to match the picture. Then have them tell how the picture and equation show 10 ones and some more ones.

2

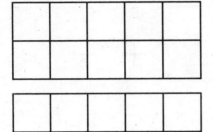

$$13 = \text{\_\_\_\_} + \text{\_\_\_\_}$$

3

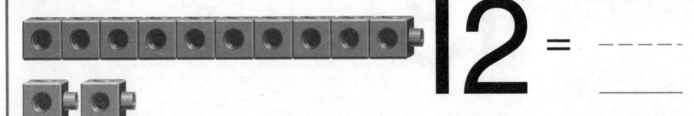

$$12 = \text{\_\_\_\_} + \text{\_\_\_\_}$$

4

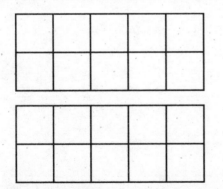

$$11 = 10 + 1$$

Directions   Have students: **2** use counters to show 13, draw them in the double ten-frame, and complete the equation to match the picture. Then have them tell how the picture and equation show 10 ones and some more ones; **3** look at the picture of 12 cubes, and complete the equation to match the picture. Then have them tell how the picture and equation show 10 ones and some more ones; **4** draw counters to match the equation. Then have them tell how the picture and equation show 10 ones and some more ones.

Independent Practice

 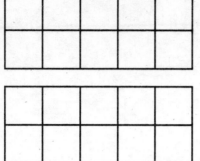

$12 =$ _____ $+$ _____

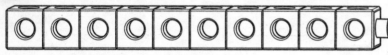

$13 =$ _____ $+$ _____

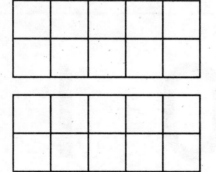

_____

_____ $=$ _____ $+$ _____

_____

_____ $+$ _____ $=$ _____

Directions Have students: draw counters to make 12, and complete the equation to match the picture. Then have them tell how the picture and equation show 10 ones and some more ones; color the cubes blue and red to make 13, and complete the equation to match the picture. Then have them tell how the picture and equation show 10 ones and some more ones. **Higher Order Thinking** Have students draw counters to show 11 and write two equations to match the picture. Then have them tell how the picture and equations show 10 ones and some more ones.

 Topic 10 | Lesson 4

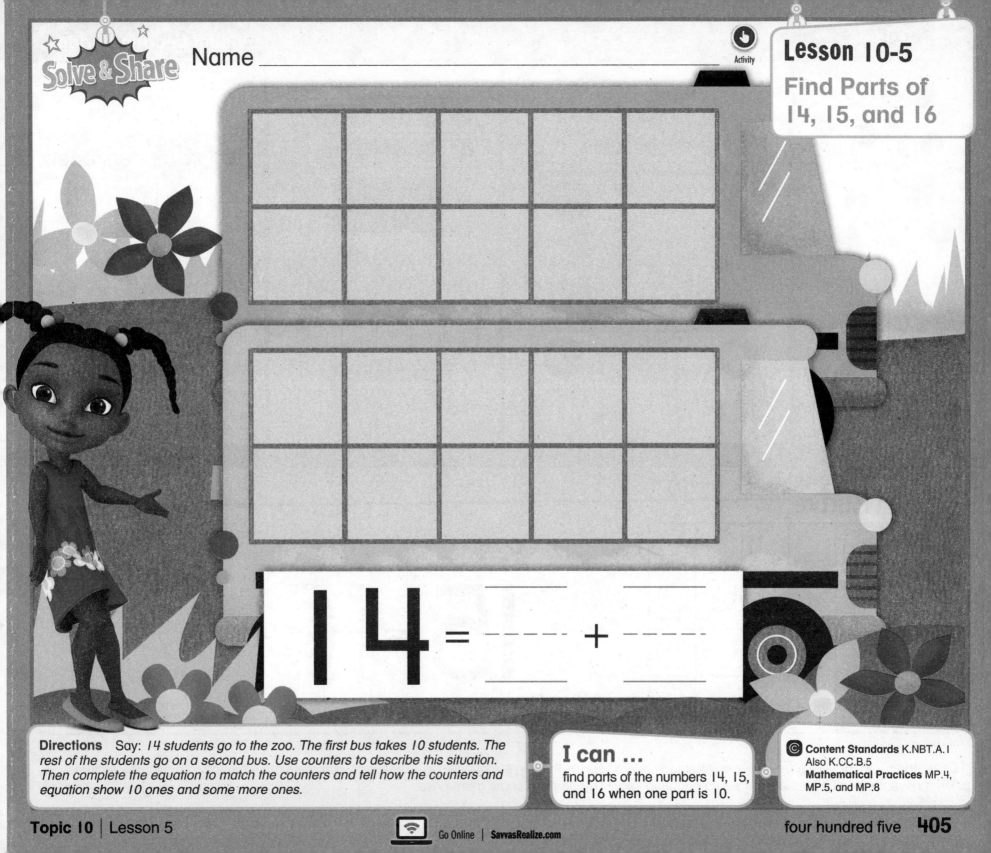

Solve & Share

Name _____

Activity

$$14 = \underline{\hspace{2cm}} + \underline{\hspace{2cm}}$$

Directions Say: 14 students go to the zoo. The first bus takes 10 students. The rest of the students go on a second bus. Use counters to describe this situation. Then complete the equation to match the counters and tell how the counters and equation show 10 ones and some more ones.

I can ...
find parts of the numbers 14, 15, and 16 when one part is 10.

© **Content Standards** K.NBT.A.1 Also K.CC.B.5 **Mathematical Practices** MP.4, MP.5, and MP.8

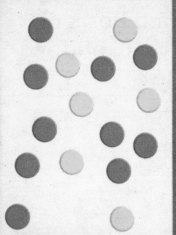

16

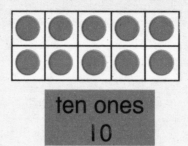
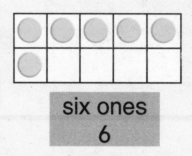

ten ones
10

six ones
6

ten ones   six ones

16 = 10 + 6

☆ Guided Practice

1

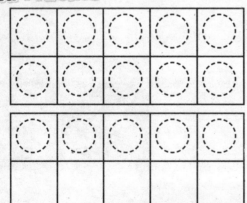

15 = 10 + 5

Directions 1 Have students use counters to show 15, draw them in the double ten-frame, and complete the equation to match the picture. Then have them tell how the picture and equation show 10 ones and some more ones.

Topic 10 | Lesson 5

Name _____

2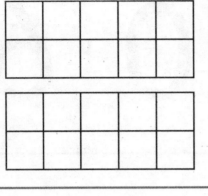

$$14 = \text{\_\_\_\_} + \text{\_\_\_\_}$$

3

$$16 = \text{\_\_\_\_} + \text{\_\_\_\_}$$

4

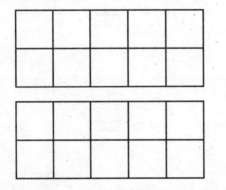

$$15 = 10 + 5$$

Directions Have students: **2** use counters to show 14, draw them in the double ten-frame, and complete the equation to match the picture. Then have them tell how the picture and equation show 10 ones and some more ones; **3** look at the picture of 16 cubes, and complete the equation to match the picture. Then have them tell how the picture and equation show 10 ones and some more ones; **4** draw counters to match the equation. Then have them tell how the picture and equation show 10 ones and some more ones.

Independent Practice

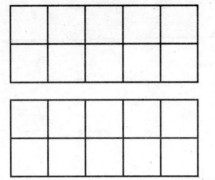

$$16 = 10 + 6$$

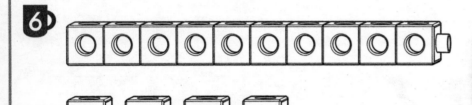

$$14 = \underline{\quad\quad} + \underline{\quad\quad}$$

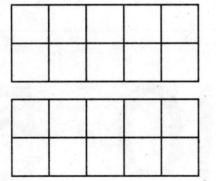

$$\underline{\quad\quad} = \underline{\quad\quad} + \underline{\quad\quad}$$

$$\underline{\quad\quad} \qquad \underline{\quad\quad} \qquad \underline{\quad\quad}$$

$$\underline{\quad\quad} + \underline{\quad\quad} = \underline{\quad\quad}$$

$$\underline{\quad\quad} \qquad \underline{\quad\quad} \qquad \underline{\quad\quad}$$

Directions Have students ✋ draw counters to match the equation. Then have them tell how the picture and equation show 10 ones and some more ones. ☕ color the cubes blue and red to show 14, complete the equation to match the picture, and tell how the picture and equation show 10 ones and some more ones. 🌲 **Higher Order Thinking** Have students use counters to show 16, draw them in the double ten-frame, and complete two equations to match the picture. Then have them tell how the picture and equations show 10 ones and some more ones.

   Topic 10 | Lesson 5

Name _____

$$\boxed{} = \boxed{} + \boxed{}$$

I can ...
find parts of the numbers
17, 18, and 19 when one part
is 10.

© **Content Standards** K.NBT.A.1
Also K.CC.B.5
Mathematical Practices MP.1,
MP.4, and MP.8

Directions Say: *How can these 18 boxes be split into ten ones and some more ones? Use 2 different color crayons to color the boxes to show your work. Then write an equation to match the picture.*

17

7
10

10

7

17 = 10 + 7

☆ Guided Practice

1 18 = 10 + 8

410 four hundred ten

Topic 10 | Lesson 6

Name _____

2

____ ____ ____

- - - - - = - - - - - + - - - - -

____ ____ ____

3

____ ____ ____

- - - - - = - - - - - + - - - - -

____ ____ ____

4

$18 = $ - - - - - + - - - - -

Directions Have students: **2** and **3** color 10 squares blue to show 10 ones, and then draw 10 blue squares in the top ten-frame. Have them color the remaining cubes in the train red to show more ones, count them, and then draw red squares in the bottom ten-frame. Then have them write an equation to match the pictures; **4** complete the equation to match the counters. Then have them tell how the picture and equation show 10 ones and some more ones.

Topic 10 | Lesson 6
four hundred eleven **411**

Independent Practice

Tools   Assessment

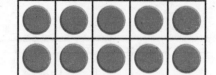
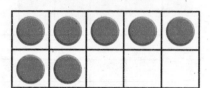

$$17 = \underline{\hspace{2cm}} + \underline{\hspace{2cm}}$$

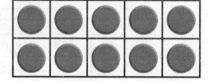
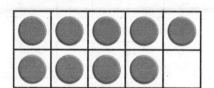

$$19 = \underline{\hspace{2cm}} + \underline{\hspace{2cm}}$$

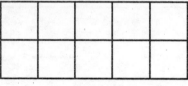
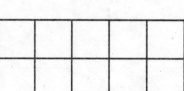

$$\underline{\hspace{2cm}} = \underline{\hspace{2cm}} + \underline{\hspace{2cm}}$$

$$\underline{\hspace{2cm}} + \underline{\hspace{2cm}} = \underline{\hspace{2cm}}$$

Directions ✋ and 🥤 Have students complete the equation to match the counters. Then have them tell how the picture and equation show 10 ones and some more ones. 🌲 **Higher Order Thinking** Have students use counters to show 18, draw them in the double ten-frame, and write two equations to match the picture. Then have them tell how the picture and equations show 10 ones and some more ones.

       Topic 10 | Lesson 6

Name _____

Activity

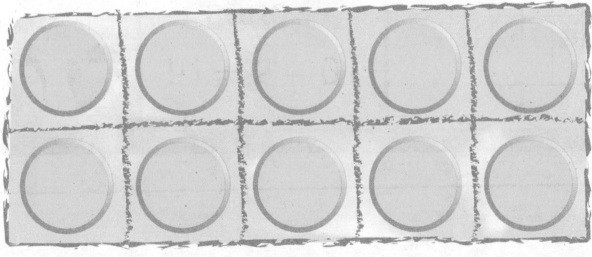

Directions Say: *Put some counters in the red five-frame. Use a red crayon and write the number that tells how many counters are in the red frame. Put the same number of counters in the blue five-frame. Use a blue crayon and write the number that tells how many counters are in the blue frames. Show the numbers to a partner. Compare your answers and look for patterns. How is your blue number like your red number? How is it different?*

I can ...
look for patterns to make and find the parts of numbers to 19.

© **Mathematical Practices** MP.7
Also MP.3, MP.8
Content Standards K.NBT.A.1
Also K.CC.B.5

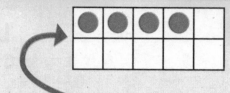

What is the pattern?

1	2	3	4	5	6	7	8	9	10
11	12	13	14	15	16	17	18	19	20

4 ones

_____

1 ten
+
4 ones

$10 + 4 = 14$

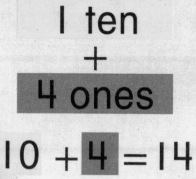
4 / 14
5 / 15
6 / 16

10 greater than

⭐ Guided Practice

1

1	2	3	4	5	6	7	8	9	10
11	12	13	14	15	16	17	18	19	20

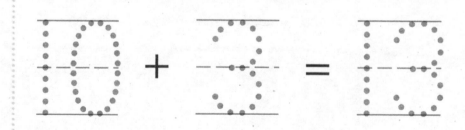

10 + 3 = 13

Directions ⭐ Have students find the number with the blue box around it, and then color the number that is 10 greater than the number in the blue box. Have them write an equation to show how the teen number they colored is composed of 10 ones and some more ones. Then have students explain how they decided what parts to add to make the teen number.

414 four hundred fourteen

Topic 10 | Lesson 7

Name _____

Independent Practice

2

1	2	3	4	5	6	7	8	9	10
11	12	13	14	15	16	17	18	19	20

_____ + _____ = _____

3

1	2	3	4	5	6	7	8	9	10
11	12	13	14	15	16	17	18	19	20

_____ + _____ = _____

4

1	2	3	4	5	6	7	8	9	10
11	12	13	14	15	16	17	18	19	20

_____ + _____ = _____

5

$10 + 1 = 11$ $10 + 2 = 12$ _____ + _____ = **13**

Directions Have students: **2–4** find the number with the blue box around it, and color the number that is 10 greater than the number in the blue box. Then have them write an equation to show how the teen number they colored is composed of 10 ones and some more ones; **5** complete the equation to continue the pattern, and then explain the pattern they made.

Topic 10 | Lesson 7

four hundred fifteen **415**

Problem Solving

1	2	3	4	5	6	7	8	9	10
11	12	13	14	15	16	17	18	19	20

$$\boxed{6} \quad \rule{3cm}{0.4pt} + \rule{2cm}{0.4pt} = \rule{3cm}{0.4pt}$$

$$\boxed{7} \quad \rule{3cm}{0.4pt} + \rule{2cm}{0.4pt} = \rule{3cm}{0.4pt}$$

Directions Read the problem to students. Then have them use multiple problem-solving methods to solve the problem. Say: *Mr. Shepard's class will exchange cards at a holiday party. There are 16 students in the class. The store sells cards in packs of 10. Alex already has 6 cards. Marta already has 7 cards. How many cards will Alex and Marta have after they each buy one pack of cards?* ⓺ **Use Structure** *How can the number chart help you solve the problem? Write the equations for the number of cards Alex and Marta will have.* ⓻ **Generalize** *After you find the number of cards Alex will have, is it easier to find the number of cards Marta will have?* ⓼ **Explain** *Tell a friend why your answers are correct. Then tell the friend about the pattern you see in the number chart and how the equations show 10 ones and some more ones.*

1

O	G	H
2 + 3	4 − 2	5 − 2

4 − 1	4 + 1	1 + 1

2

W	C	O
2 − 1	2 + 2	1 − 1

1 + 3	0 + 0	5 − 4

Directions 1 and 2 Have students find a partner. Have them point to a clue in the top row, and then solve the addition or subtraction problem. Then have them look at the clues in the bottom row to find a match, and then write the clue letter above the match. Have students find a match for every clue.

I can ...
add and subtract fluently within 5.

© **Content Standard** K.OA.A.5
Mathematical Practices MP.3, MP.6, MP.7, and MP.8

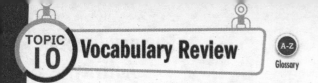

$$10 + \underline{\hspace{2cm}} = 15$$

$$19 = 10 + \underline{\hspace{2cm}}$$

Directions **Understand Vocabulary** Have students: ☆ complete the drawing and the equation to show **how many more** counters are needed to make 15; ② complete the drawing and the equation to show **how many more** counters are needed to make 19.

Name _____

Set A

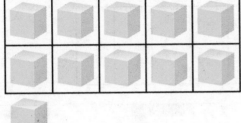

⭐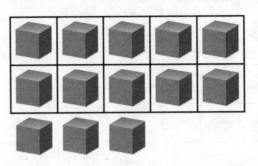

$$10 + 1 = 11$$

_____ + _____ = _____

Set B

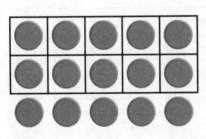

②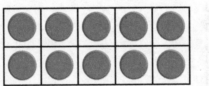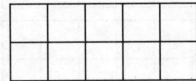

$$10 + 5 = 15$$

_____ + _____ = _____

Directions Have students: ⭐ write an equation to match the blocks. Then have them tell how the picture and equation show 10 ones and some more ones; ② draw counters to show 16, and then write an equation to match the picture. Then tell how the picture and equation show 10 ones and some more ones.

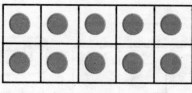

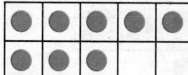

$$10 + 8 = 18$$

❸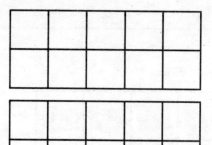

$$10 + 7 = 17$$

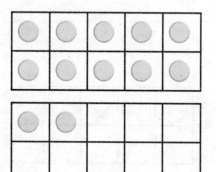

$$12 = 10 + 2$$

❹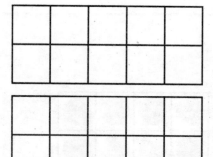

$$11 = \text{\_\_\_} + \text{\_\_\_}$$

Directions Have students: **❸** draw counters to match the equation. Then have them tell how the picture and equation show 10 ones and some more ones; **❹** draw counters to make 11, and then complete the equation to match the picture. Then have them tell how the picture and equation show 10 ones and some more ones.

420 four hundred twenty

Name _____

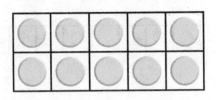

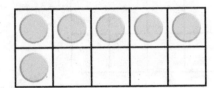

$16 = 10 + 6$

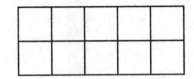

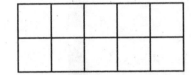

$14 = \text{------} + \text{------}$

| 1 | 2 | 3 | 4 | 5 | 6 | 7 | 8 | 9 | 10 |
| 11 | 12 | 13 | 14 | 15 | 16 | 17 | 18 | 19 | 20 |

| 1 | 2 | 3 | 4 | 5 | 6 | 7 | 8 | 9 | 10 |
| 11 | 12 | 13 | 14 | 15 | 16 | 17 | 18 | 19 | 20 |

$19 = 10 + 9$

$\text{------} + \text{------} = \text{------}$

Directions Have students: ✋ use counters to show 14, draw them in the double ten-frame, and complete the equation to match the picture. Then have them tell how the picture and equation show 10 ones and some more ones; ☕ find the number with the blue box around it, and color the number that is 10 greater than the number in the blue box. Then have them write an equation to match, and then tell how the equation shows 10 ones and some more ones.

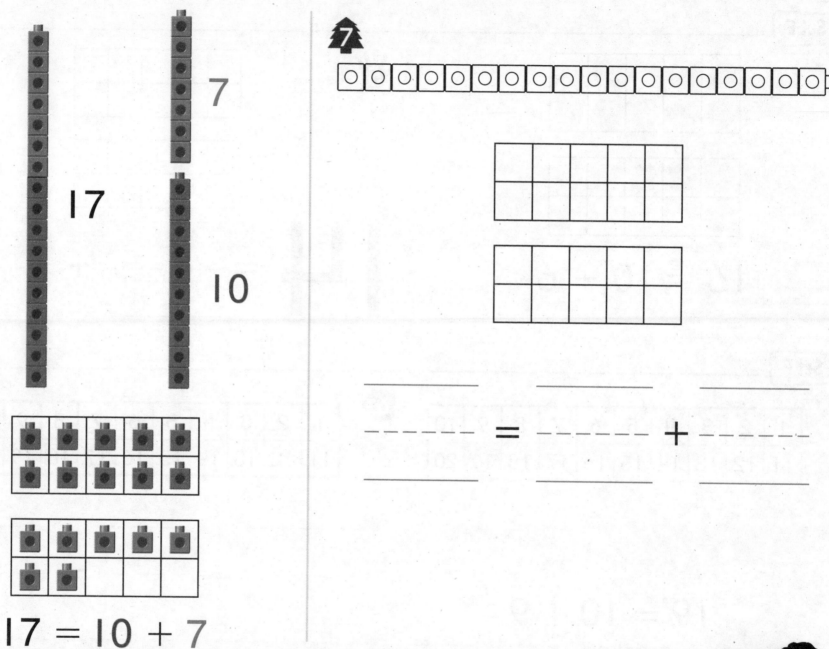

17

7

10

17 = 10 + 7

_____ _____ _____

— — — — = — — — — + — — — —

_____ _____ _____

Directions Have students: 🌲 color 10 cubes blue in the train to show 10 ones, and then draw 10 blue cubes in the top ten-frame. Have them color the remaining cubes in the train red to show more ones, count them, and then draw the same number of red cubes in the bottom ten-frame. Then have them write an equation to match the pictures.

Name _____

 1

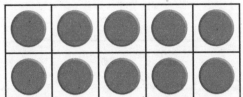

Ⓐ $15 = 10 + 5$

Ⓑ $14 = 10 + 4$

Ⓒ $13 = 10 + 3$

Ⓓ $12 = 10 + 2$

 2

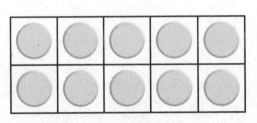

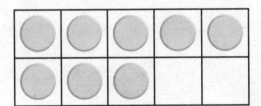

Ⓐ 10 and 6

Ⓑ 10 and 7

Ⓒ 10 and 8

Ⓓ 10 and 9

_____ + _____ = 18

3

Ⓐ 10 and 0

Ⓑ 10 and 1

Ⓒ 10 and 2

Ⓓ 10 and 3

Directions Have students mark the best answer. ⭐ Say: *Mason uses counters in ten-frames to count his marbles. Which equation matches the picture and shows how many marbles Mason has?* 🍎 Say: *Sarah counts the number of counters and gets 18. Which two numbers add to 18? Use the equation and double ten-frame for help.* 🎯 Say: *Cole has 12 toy trucks. How can Cole split up his trucks into ten ones and some more ones?*

4

1	2	3	4	5	6	7	8	9	10
11	12	13	14	15	16	17	18	19	20

_____ _____ _____

_ _ _ _ _ **+** _ _ _ _ _ **=** _ _ _ _ _

5

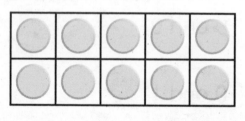

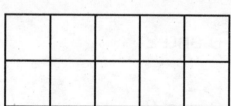

$13 =$ _ _ _ _ _ **+** _ _ _ _ _

Directions Have students: ❤ find the number with the blue box around it, and then color the number that is 10 greater than the number in the blue box. Then have them write an equation that shows how the teen number they colored is composed of ten and some more ones; ✋ draw counters to make 13, and then complete the equation to match the picture.

6

$$10 + 6 = 16$$

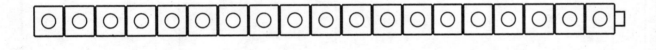

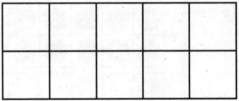

_ _ _ _ _ = _ _ _ _ _ + _ _ _ _ _

_ _ _ _ _

Directions Have students: **6** listen to this story: *Gabby has 16 counters. She wants to put her counters into a double ten-frame in order to decompose 16 into tens and ones. Draw counters to match Gabby's equation.* **7** color 10 cubes blue to show 10 ones, and then draw 10 blue cubes in the top ten-frame. Have them color the remaining cubes in the train red to show more ones, count them, and then draw the same number of red cubes in the bottom ten-frame. Then have them write an equation to match the pictures.

8

	$14 = 10 + 4$	$11 = 10 + 1$	$13 = 10 + 3$	$17 = 10 + 7$
(ten-frame: 13)	☐	☐	☐	☐
(ten-frame: 17)	☐	☐	☐	☐
(ten-frame: 11)	☐	☐	☐	☐
(ten-frame: 14)	☐	☐	☐	☐

Directions **8** Have students choose the equation that matches each double ten-frame.

Topic 10 | Assessment Practice

Name _____

⭐ 1

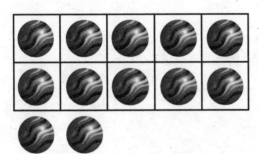

_____ _____ _____

_ _ _ _ _   +   _ _ _ _ _   =   _ _ _ _ _

🍎 2

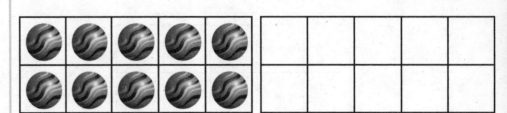

18 = _ _ _ _ _   +   _ _ _ _ _

 3

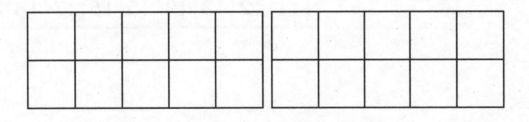

_____ _____ _____

_ _ _ _ _   =   _ _ _ _ _   +   _ _ _ _ _   _ _ _ _ _   +   _ _ _ _ _   =   _ _ _ _ _

Directions   Mason's Marbles Say: *Mason collects many different kinds of marbles. He uses ten-frames to help count his marbles.* Have students: ⭐ write the equation to show how many purple marbles Mason has; 🍎 draw red marbles in the second ten-frame to show 18 red marbles in all, and then complete the equation. Have them tell how the picture and equation show 10 ones and some more ones; ✖ draw 17 yellow marbles in the double ten-frame, and then write two equations to match their drawing.

♥ 4

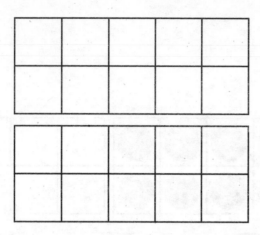

$$10 + 3 = 13$$

1	2	3	4	5	6	7	8	9	10
11	12	13	14	15	16	17	18	19	20

_____   _____   _____

\- - - - - **+** - - - - **=** - - - - -

_____   _____   _____

Directions ♥ Have students look at the equation Mason wrote to show how many green marbles he has, and then draw the marbles in the double ten-frame to show the number. Have them tell how the picture shows 10 ones and some more ones. ✋ Say: *Mason put his striped marbles in a five-frame. Then he buys 10 more striped marbles.* Have students write the number to tell how many striped marbles Mason had at first, and then color the part of the number chart to show how many striped marbles he has now. Then have them write an equation and ask them to explain how the picture and equation show 10 ones and some more ones.

 Topic 10 | Performance Task

Essential Question: How can numbers to 100 be counted using a hundred chart?

Digital Resources

Interactive Student Edition   Activity   Visual Learning   Video   Practice

Assessment   Games   Tools   Glossary

Ants

Ants live in colonies.

enVision STEM Project: Ant Colonies

Directions Read the character speech bubbles to students. **Find Out!** Have students find out how ants live and work together in colonies.
Say: *Talk to friends and relatives about ant colonies. Ask about the different jobs ants in a colony might have that help them survive.* **Journal: Make a Poster** Have students make a poster. Have them draw an ant colony with 5 groups of ants. There should be 10 ants in each group. Then have them count by tens to find how many ants there are in all. Have students use a hundred chart to practice counting by tens to 50.

Name _____

 Review What You Know

1

11 17 19

2

10 + 6

3 + 10

3

10 + 4

8 + 10

4

_ _ _ _ _ _ _ _ _ _

_ _ _ _ _ _ _ _ _ _

5

_ _ _ _ _ _ _ _ _ _

_ _ _ _ _ _ _ _ _ _

6

_ _ _ _ _ _ _ _ _ _

_ _ _ _ _ _ _ _ _ _

Directions Have students: **1** draw a circle around the number *nineteen*; **2** draw a circle around the addition expression that makes 16; **3** draw a circle around the addition expression that makes 18; **4**–**6** count each set of objects, write the numbers to tell how many, and then draw a circle around the number that is greater than the other number.

Name _____

Pick a Project

A

B

C

Directions Say: *You will choose one of these projects. Look at picture A. Think about this question: What if you had more than two legs? If you choose Project A, you will make a model of a centipede. Look at picture B. Think about this question: Is there any math in dancing? If you choose Project B, you will create a numbers dance. Look at picture C. Think about this question: Where can you find a moonstone? If you choose Project C, you will collect and count treasures.*

I can do that, too!

Directions Read the robot's speech bubble to students. **Generate Interest** Ask students about their experience stacking blocks. Say: *What's the tallest block tower you have built? How many blocks was it?* Give students a chance to practice building block towers and observe how many blocks tall they are.

I can ...

model with math to count by 1s and 10s to solve a problem.

© **Mathematical Practices** MP.4
Also MP.3, MP.5
Content Standards K.CC.A.1
Also K.CC.A.2

Topic 11 | 3-Act Math

Name _____

1	2	3	4	5	6	7	8	9	10
11	12	13	14	15	16	17	18	19	20
21	22	23	24	25	26	27	28	29	30

Directions Say: *Count forward from 1 to 30. Count aloud and point to each number as you say it. What patterns do you see or hear when you count to 30 using the numbers on the chart? Color the boxes that show a pattern you find.*

I can ...
use patterns to count to 30.

Content Standards K.CC.A.1
Also K.CC.A.2
Mathematical Practices MP.2, MP.6, and MP.7

 Guided Practice

1

1	2	3	4	5	6	7	8	9	10

2

11	12	13	14	15	16	17	18	19	20
21	22	23	24	25	26	27	28	29	30

Directions Have students: **1** count forward from 1 to 10. Count aloud and point to each number as it is said. Have them listen to the following numbers in the bottom row, and then draw a circle around the number in the top row and the part of the number in the bottom row that sound alike: *twenty-ONE, twenty-TWO, twenty-THREE, twenty-FOUR, twenty-FIVE, twenty-SIX*. **2** listen to the pattern, and then use crayons to color the numbers that they hear: 16, 17, 18, 19.

 Topic 11 | Lesson 1

Name _____

3

1	2	3	4	5	6	7	8	9	10
11	12	13	14	15	16	17	18	19	20
21	22	23	24	25	26	27	28	29	30

4

5

1	2	3	4	5	6	7	8	9	10
11	12	13	14	15	16	17	18	19	20
21	22	23	24	25	26	27	28	29	30

6

Directions Have students listen to the count, color the numbers they hear, and then tell what pattern they see or hear: **3** 1, 2, 3, 4, 5; **4** 25, 26, 27, 28; **5** 4, 14, 24; **6** 16, 17, 18, 19.

Independent Practice

7

1	2	3	4	5	6	7	8	9	10
11	12	13	14	15	16	17	18	19	20
21	22	23	24	25	26	27	28	29	30

8

9

1	2	3	4	5	6	7	8	9	10
11	12	13	14	15	16	17	18	19	20
21	22	23	24	25	26	27	28	29	30

Directions Have students listen to the count, color the numbers they hear, and then tell what pattern they see or hear: 🎄 7, 17, 27; 🚩 21, 22, 23, 24, 25. ◆ **Higher Order Thinking** Have students listen to the count, color the numbers they hear, and then tell what pattern they hear: 13, 14, 15, 16, 17, 18. Then have them draw a circle around the next number in the pattern.

   Topic 11 | Lesson 1

Name _____

 Activity

Solve & Share

1	2	3	4	5	6	7	8	9	10
11	12	13	14	15	16	17	18	19	20
21	22	23	24	25	26	27	28	29	30
31	32	33	34	35	36	37	38	39	40
41	42	43	44	45	46	47	48	49	50

Directions Say: *Work with a partner. Count forward from 1 to 50. One partner points to each number in the first row while the other partner counts aloud each number. Change jobs for every row. Watch students go through all 5 rows.* Say: *Now, one partner will cover some numbers on the board using counters. The other partner will name the hidden numbers. Play 3 times, and then color the numbers that are the hardest to remember.*

I can ...
use patterns to count to 50.

© **Content Standards** K.CC.A.1
Also K.CC.A.2
Mathematical Practices MP.1,
MP.6, and MP.8

1	2	3	4	5	6	7	8	9	●
11	12	13	14	15	16	17	18	19	●
21	22	23	24	25	26	27	28	29	●
31	32	33	34	35	36	37	38	39	●
41	42	43	44	45	46	47	48	49	●

1	2	3	4	5	6	7	8	9	10
11	12	13	14	15	16	17	18	19	20
21	22	23	24	25	26	27	28	29	30
31	32	33	○	○	○	○	○	39	40
41	42	43	44	45	46	47	48	49	50

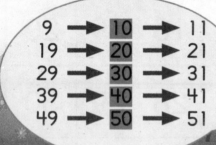

9 → **10** → 11
19 → **20** → 21
29 → **30** → 31
39 → **40** → 41
49 → **50** → 51

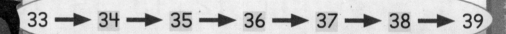
33 → 34 → 35 → 36 → 37 → 38 → 39

☆ Guided Practice

21	22	23	24	25	26	27	28	29	30
31	32	33	34	35	36	37	38	39	40
41	42	43	44	45	46	47	48	49	50

Directions Have students: ⭐ count aloud the numbers in the top row and point to each number as it is said. Then have them count aloud the numbers in the middle row beginning with 31 and ending with 39, and draw a circle around the part of the number that sounds the same; 🍎 read the numbers in the first column. Draw a circle around the number that you hear in each number.

Name _____

1	2	3	4	5	6	7	8	9	10
11	12	13	14	15	16	17	18	19	20
21	22	23	24	25	26	27	28	29	30
31	32	33	34	35	36	37	38	39	40
41	42	43	44	45	46	47	48	49	50

Directions Have students: ❸ find the green number on the chart, and then begin counting forward by ones up to 30. Say: *Color green all the numbers that have "twenty" as part of the number;* ❹ Find the red number and begin counting forward by ones and stop when they get to 49. Say: *Color red all the numbers you counted;* ❺ find the yellow number. Then have them count forward by ones until they get to the red number. Say: *What numbers did you count? Color them yellow;* ❻ find the blue number. Then draw a circle around the parts of the numbers in the column that are the same; ❼ use counters to cover 3 numbers on the chart. Say: *Show your chart to a friend, and ask them to tell you which numbers are hiding.*

Independent Practice

1	2	3	4	5	6	7	8	9	10
11	12	13	14	15	16	17	18	19	20
21	22	23	24	25	26	27	28	29	30
31	32	33	34	35	36	37	38	39	40
41	42	43	44	45	46	47	48	49	50

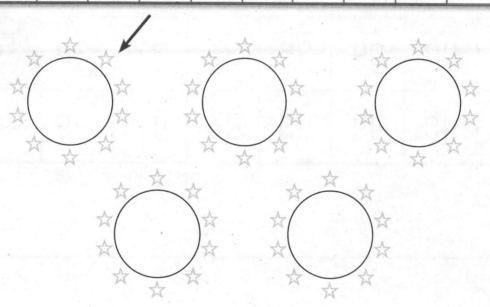

8

9

Directions 8 Have students begin counting stars around the first circle at the arrow, and continue clockwise around the circle until they have counted all the stars. Say: *When you finish counting one circle, cross off the last number you said in your count on the chart.* Have students continue counting the stars around the circles, crossing off the last number they said in each circle, until they reach the end of the stars. 9 **Higher Order Thinking** Say: *Color one number in the chart. Now count that same number of stars below. Color each star to show how many you counted.*

1	2	3	4	5	6	7	8	9	10
11	12	13	14	15	16	17	18	19	20
21	22	23	24	25	26	27	28	29	30
31	32	33	34	35	36	37	38	39	40
41	42	43	44	45	46	47	48	49	50
51	52	53	54	55	56	57	58	59	60
61	62	63	64	65	66	67	68	69	70
71	72	73	74	75	76	77	78	79	80
81	82	83	84	85	86	87	88	89	90
91	92	93	94	95	96	97	98	99	100

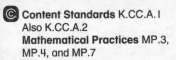

Directions Say: *Color all the boxes of the numbers that have a zero as you count them aloud. Tell how you know which numbers to count. Count forward by tens beginning at 30 and going to 100. Point to the numbers as you count them aloud to a partner. Now begin at 60. Count forward by tens to 100. Mark each number with an X as you say it to your partner.*

I can ...
skip count by tens to 100.

© **Content Standards** K.CC.A.1 Also K.CC.A.2 **Mathematical Practices** MP.3, MP.4, and MP.7

Visual Learning Bridge

1	2	3	4	5	6	7	8	9	10
11	12	13	14	15	16	17	18	19	20
21	22	23	24	25	26	27	28	29	30
31	32	33	34	35	36	37	38	39	40
41	42	43	44	45	46	47	48	49	50
51	52	53	54	55	56	57	58	59	60

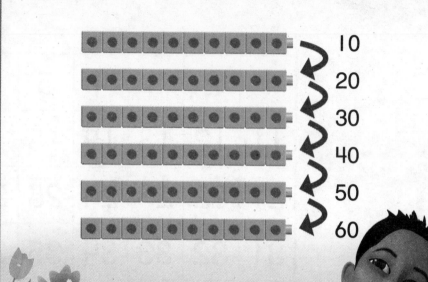

10
20
30
40
50
60

☆ Guided Practice

1

1	2	3	4	5	6	7	8	9	10
11	12	13	14	15	16	17	18	19	20
21	22	23	24	25	26	27	28	29	(30)
31	32	33	34	35	36	37	38	39	40
41	42	43	44	45	46	47	48	49	50
51	52	53	54	55	56	57	58	59	60

2

51	52	53	54	55	56	57	58	59	60
61	62	63	64	65	66	67	68	69	(70)
71	72	73	74	75	76	77	78	79	80
81	82	83	84	85	86	87	88	89	90
91	92	93	94	95	96	97	98	99	100

Directions Have students: **1** draw a circle around the decade number that comes before 40 but after 20; **2** circle the decade number that is missing from this pattern: 60, 80, 90, 100.

442 four hundred forty-two

Topic 11 | Lesson 3

Name _____

3
1	2	3	4	5	6	7	8	9	10
11	12	13	14	15	16	17	18	19	20
21	22	23	24	25	26	27	28	29	30
31	32	33	34	35	36	37	38	39	40
41	42	43	44	45	46	47	48	49	50
51	52	53	54	55	56	57	58	59	60
61	62	63	64	65	66	67	68	69	70
71	72	73	74	75	76	77	78	79	80
81	82	83	84	85	86	87	88	89	90
91	92	93	94	95	96	97	98	99	100

4

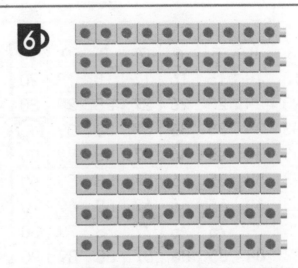

20 30 50

5

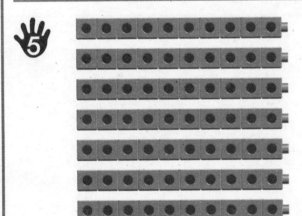

40 60 70

6

80 90 100

Directions Have students: **3** draw a circle around the missing numbers in the following pattern: *ten, twenty, thirty,* ____, *fifty,* ____, *seventy,* ____, ____, *one hundred;* **4**–**6** count the cubes by tens, and then draw a circle around the number that tells how many.

Independent Practice

Tools Assessment

7

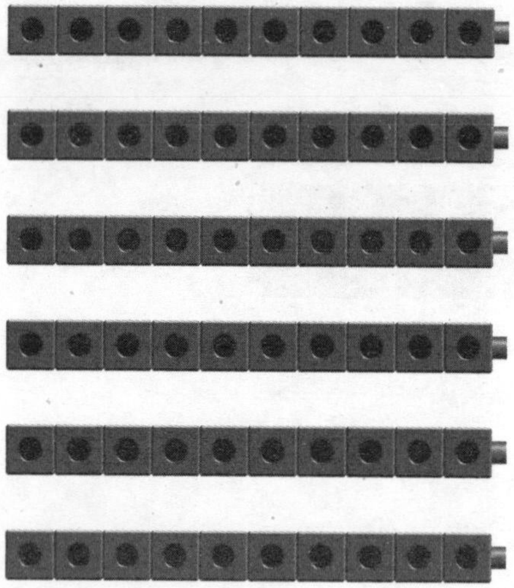

60 80 100

8

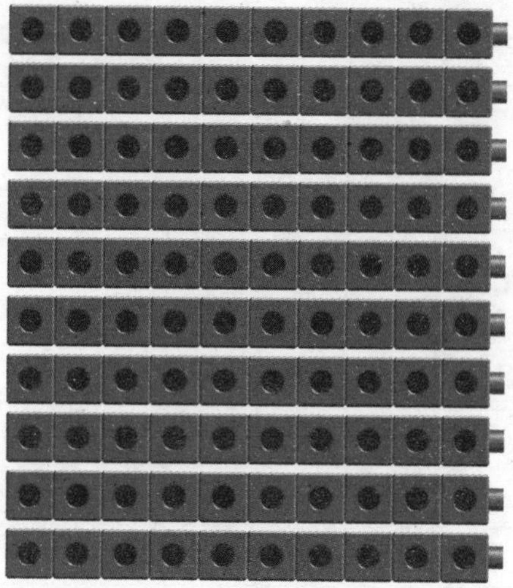

60 80 100

9

1	2	3	4	5	6	7	8	9	10
11	12	13	14	15	16	17	18	19	20
21	22	23	24	25	26	27	28	29	30
31	32	33	34	35	36	37	38	39	40
41	42	43	44	45	46	47	48	49	50
51	52	53	54	55	56	57	58	59	60
61	62	63	64	65	66	67	68	69	70
71	72	73	74	75	76	77	78	79	80
81	82	83	84	85	86	87	88	89	90
91	92	93	94	95	96	97	98	99	100

10

Directions 7–8 Have students count the cubes, and then draw a circle around the number that tells how many. 9 Say: *If you start with 40, how would you count to 100 by tens? Circle the numbers you count.* 10 **Higher Order Thinking** Have students look at the hundred chart and read the decade numbers. Say: *How many decade numbers are there in the chart? Write the number.*

1	2	3	4	5	6	7	8	9	10
11	12	13	14	15	16	17	18	19	20
21	22	23	24	25	26	27	28	29	30
31	32	33	34	35	36	37	38	39	40
41	42	43	44	45	46	47	48	49	50
51	52	53	54	55	56	57	58	59	60
61	62	63	64	65	66	67	68	69	70
71	72	73	74	75	76	77	78	79	80
81	82	83	84	85	86	87	88	89	90
91	92	93	94	95	96	97	98	99	100

Directions Say: *Count forward from the yellow number. Stop at the red number. Tell how many numbers you counted aloud. Color the boxes of the numbers you counted aloud to show your work.* Have students repeat the same steps for the blue to green sequence of squares, and for the orange to purple sequence of squares.

I can ...

count forward from any number to 100 by ones.

© **Content Standards** K.CC.A.2 Also K.CC.A.1 **Mathematical Practices** MP.5, MP.7, and MP.8

72

91

71	72	73	74	75	76	77	78	79	80
81	82	83	84	85	86	87	88	89	90
91	92	93	94	95	96	97	98	99	100

☆ Guided Practice

 1

21	22	23	24	25	26	27	28	29	30
31	32	33	34	35	36	37	38	39	40
41	42	43	44	45	46	47	48	49	50
51	52	53	54	55	56	57	58	59	60

2

1	2	3	4	5	6	7	8	9	10
11	12	13	14	15	16	17	18	19	20
21	22	23	24	25	26	27	28	29	30
31	32	33	34	35	36	37	38	39	40

Directions 🏠 **1** and **2** Have students color the boxes of the numbers as they count aloud, starting at the yellow box and ending at the red box.

3

1	2	3	4	5	6	7	8	9	10
11	12	13	14	15	16	17	18	19	20
21	22	23	24	25	26	27	28	29	30
31	32	33	34	35	36	37	38	39	40
41	42	43	44	45	46	47	48	49	50
51	52	53	54	55	56	57	58	59	60
61	62	63	64	65	66	67	68	69	70
71	72	73	74	75	76	77	78	79	80
81	82	83	84	85	86	87	88	89	90
91	92	93	94	95	96	97	98	99	100

 4

1	2	3	4	5	6	7	8	9	10
11	12	13	14	15	16	17	18	19	20
21	22	23	24	25	26	27	28	29	30
31	32	33	34	35	36	37	38	39	40
41	42	43	44	45	46	47	48	49	50
51	52	53	54	55	56	57	58	59	60
61	62	63	64	65	66	67	68	69	70
71	72	73	74	75	76	77	78	79	80
81	82	83	84	85	86	87	88	89	90
91	92	93	94	95	96	97	98	99	100

 5

1	2	3	4	5	6	7	8	9	10
11	12	13	14	15	16	17	18	19	20
21	22	23	24	25	26	27	28	29	30
31	32	33	34	35	36	37	38	39	40
41	42	43	44	45	46	47	48	49	50
51	52	53	54	55	56	57	58	59	60
61	62	63	64	65	66	67	68	69	70
71	72	73	74	75	76	77	78	79	80
81	82	83	84	85	86	87	88	89	90
91	92	93	94	95	96	97	98	99	100

 6

1	2	3	4	5	6	7	8	9	10
11	12	13	14	15	16	17	18	19	20
21	22	23	24	25	26	27	28	29	30
31	32	33	34	35	36	37	38	39	40
41	42	43	44	45	46	47	48	49	50
51	52	53	54	55	56	57	58	59	60
61	62	63	64	65	66	67	68	69	70
71	72	73	74	75	76	77	78	79	80
81	82	83	84	85	86	87	88	89	90
91	92	93	94	95	96	97	98	99	100

Directions **3–6** Have students color the boxes of the numbers as they count aloud, starting at the yellow box and ending at the red box.

Independent Practice

 7

1	2	3	4	5	6	7	8	9	10
11	12	13	14	15	16	17	18	19	20
21	22	23	24	25	26	27	28	29	30
31	32	33	34	35	36	37	38	39	40
41	42	43	44	45	46	47	48	49	50
51	52	53	54	55	56	57	58	59	60
61	62	63	64	65	66	67	68	69	70
71	72	73	74	75	76	77	78	79	80
81	82	83	84	85	86	87	88	89	90
91	92	93	94	95	96	97	98	99	100

 8

1	2	3	4	5	6	7	8	9	10
11	12	13	14	15	16	17	18	19	20
21	22	23	24	25	26	27	28	29	30
31	32	33	34	35	36	37	38	39	40
41	42	43	44	45	46	47	48	49	50
51	52	53	54	55	56	57	58	59	60
61	62	63	64	65	66	67	68	69	70
71	72	73	74	75	76	77	78	79	80
81	82	83	84	85	86	87	88	89	90
91	92	93	94	95	96	97	98	99	100

 9

1	2	3	4	5	6	7	8	9	10
11	12	13	14	15	16	17	18	19	20
21	22	23	24	25	26	27	28	29	30
31	32	33	34	35	36	37	38	39	40
41	42	43	44	45	46	47	48	49	50
51	52	53	54	55	56	57	58	59	60
61	62	63	64	65	66	67	68	69	70
71	72	73	74	75	76	77	78	79	80
81	82	83	84	85	86	87	88	89	90
91	92	93	94	95	96	97	98	99	100

 10

1	2	3	4	5	6	7	8	9	10
11	12	13	14	15	16	17	18	19	20
21	22	23	24	25	26	27	28	29	30
31	32	33	34	35	36	37	38	39	40
41	42	43	44	45	46	47	48	49	50
51	52	53	54	55	56	57	58	59	60
61	62	63	64	65	66	67	68	69	70
71	72	73	74	75	76	77	78	79	80
81	82	83	84	85	86	87	88	89	90
91	92	93	94	95	96	97	98	99	100

Directions **7**–**9** Have students color the boxes of the numbers as they count aloud, starting at the yellow box and ending at the red box.
10 Higher Order Thinking Have students listen to the count, and then color the box of the missing number: 79, 80, 81, 83, 84, 85, 86, 87, 88.
Say: *Circle the numbers in the chart that are 1 more and 1 less than the missing number.*

Name _____

1	2	3	4	5	6	7	8	9	10
11	12	13	14	15	16	17	18	19	20
21	22	23	24	25	26	27	28	29	30
31	32	33	34	35	36	37	38	39	40
41	42	43	44	45	46	47	48	49	50
51	52	53	54	55	56	57	58	59	60
61	62	63	64	65	66	67	68	69	70
71	72	73	74	75	76	77	78	79	80
81	82	83	84	85	86	87	88	89	90
91	92	93	94	95	96	97	98	99	100

Directions Say: *Carlos looks at the chart. He knows 21 comes just after 20. Draw a circle around the numbers that come just after each decade number. How do you know you are correct? What patterns do you see?*

I can ...
see patterns when I count.

© **Mathematical Practices** MP.7
Also MP.6, MP.8
Content Standards K.CC.A.2
Also K.CC.A.1

41	42	43	44	45	46	47	48	49	50
51	52	53	54	55	56	57	58	59	60
61	62	63	64	65	66	67	68	69	70
71	72	73	74	75	76	77	78	79	80
81	82	83	84	85	86	87	88	89	90
91	92	93	94	95	96	97	98	99	100

61	62	63	64	65	66	67	68	69	70
71	72	73	74	75	76	77	78	79	80
81	82	83	84	85	86	87	88	89	90
91	92	93	94	95	96	97	98	99	100

☆ Guided Practice

1

1	2	3	4	5	6	7	8	9	10
11	12	13	14	15	16	17	18	19	20
21	22	23	24	25	26	27	28	29	30

2

1	2	3	4	5	6	7	8	9	10
11	12	13	14	15	16	17	18	19	20
21	22	23	24	25	26	27	28	29	30

Directions Have students ⭐ count forward by ones, beginning at 7 and going to 9. Have them circle the counted numbers. Then 🍎 count forward by tens, beginning at 10 and going to 30. Have them circle the counted numbers.

Name _____

3

61	62	63	64	65				69	70
71	72	73	74	75	76	77	78	79	80
81	82	83	84	85	86	87	88	89	90

66   76   86

67   68   69

66   67   68

4

		44	45	46	47	48	49	50
51	52	53	54	55	56	57	58	59	60
61	62	63	64	65	66	67	68	69	70

41   42   43

41   51   61

41   43   45

5

31	32	33	34	35	36	37	38	39	
41	42	43	44	45	46	47	48	49	
51	52	53	54	55	56	57	58	59	

40   50   60

40   41   42

38   39   40

6

11	12	13	14	15	16	17	18	19	20
21	22	23	24	25	26	27	28	29	
		33	34	35	36	37	38	39	40

20   30   40

28   29   30

30   31   32

Directions **3**–**6** Have students count forward, and then draw a circle around the row that shows the missing set of numbers.

Problem Solving

1	2	3	4	5	6	7	8	9	10
11	12	13	14	15	16	17	18	19	20
21	22	23	24	25	26	27	28	29	30
31	32	33	34	35	36	37	38	39	40

Directions Read the problem aloud. Then have students use multiple problem-solving methods to solve the problem. Say: *Start at 7 and count up 18 squares in any way you choose. Use your yellow crayon to make a path to show how you counted, and then draw a circle around the number where you ended.* 🌲 **Be Precise** *How many tens are in 18?* 🔷 **Use Structure** *What numbers would you say if you only counted by ones?* 🔷 **Generalize** *Start at 10 and count up 17 squares. On what number did you land? Would there be a different way to count that would solve the problem?*

452 four hundred fifty-two

Topic 11 | Lesson 5

①

G	B	I
4 + 1	2 + 2	3 − 1

3 + 1	4 − 2	2 + 3

②

T	A	C
0 + 3	4 − 3	5 − 5

3 − 3	5 − 4	1 + 2

Directions ① and ② Have students find a partner. Have them point to a clue in the top row, and then solve the addition or subtraction problem in the clue. Then have them look at the clues in the bottom row to find a match, and then write the clue letter above the match. Have students find a match for every clue.

I can ...
add and subtract fluently within 5.

© **Content Standard** K.OA.A.5 **Mathematical Practices** MP.3, MP.6, MP.7, and MP.8

1	2	3	4	5	6	7	8	9	10
11	12	13	14	15	16	17	18	19	20
21	22	23	24	25	26	27	28	29	30
31	32	33	34	35	36	37	38	39	40
41	42	43	44	45	46	47	48	49	50
51	52	53	54	55	56	57	58	59	60
61	62	63	64	65	66	67	68	69	70
71	72	73	74	75	76	77	78	79	80
81	82	83	84	85	86	87	88	89	90
91	92	93	94	95	96	97	98	99	100

Directions   Understand Vocabulary Have students: ⭐ draw a circle around the part of the number in the orange column that is 3 **ones**. ② draw a circle around the part of the number in the blue column that shows the **pattern** of 8 ones; ③ color the **decade** numbers red.

Name _____

①	②	③	④	⑤	⑥	⑦	⑧	⑨	⑩
⑪	⑫	⑬	⑭	⑮	⑯	⑰	⑱	⑲	20
21	22	23	24	25	26	27	28	29	30

1	2	3	4	5	6	7	8	9	10
11	12	13	14	15	16	17	18	19	20
21	22	23	24	25	26	27	28	29	30

Set B _____

41	42	43	44	45	46	47	48	49	50
51	52	53	54	55	56	57	58	59	60
61	62	63	64	65	66	67	68	69	70
71	72	73	74	75	76	77	78	79	80
81	82	83	84	85	86	87	88	89	90
91	92	93	94	95	96	97	98	99	100

❷

70

80

90

Directions Have students: ★ count aloud the numbers in the top row. Then have them count aloud the numbers in the bottom row and draw a circle around the number in the top row and the part of the number in the bottom row that sound the same; ❷ count by tens, and then draw a circle around the number that tells how many.

Set C

1	2	3	4	5	6	7	8	9	10
11	12	13	14	15	16	17	18	19	20
21	22	23	24	25	26	27	28	29	30
31	32	33	34	35	36	37	38	39	40
41	42	43	44	45	46	47	48	49	50

3

51	52	53	54	55	56	57	58	59	60
61	62	63	64	65	66	67	68	69	70
71	72	73	74	75	76	77	78	79	80
81	82	83	84	85	86	87	88	89	90
91	92	93	94	95	96	97	98	99	100

Set D

1	2	3	4	5	6	7	8	9	10
11	12	13	14	15	16	17	18	19	20
21	22	23	24	25	26	27	28	29	30
			34	35	36	37	38	39	40
41	42	43	44	45	46	47	48	49	50

31   32   33

4

51	52	53	54	55	56	57	58	59	60
61	62	63	64	65	66	67	68	69	70
71	72	73	74	75		77	78	79	80
81	82	83	84	85		87	88	89	90
91	92	93	94	95		97	98	99	100

75   76   77

76   86   90

76   86   96

Directions Have students: **3** color the boxes of the numbers as they count aloud by ones, starting at the yellow box and ending at the red box; **4** count forward, and then draw a circle around the row that shows the missing set of numbers.

Name _____

1

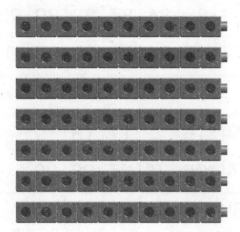

Ⓐ 60

Ⓑ 70

Ⓒ 80

Ⓓ 90

2

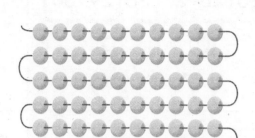

Ⓐ 56

Ⓑ 57

Ⓒ 58

Ⓓ 59

3

61	62	63	64	65	66	67	68	69	70
71	72	73	74	75	76	77	78	79	
81	82	83	84	85	86	87	88	89	
91	92	93	94	95	96	97	98	99	

Ⓐ 80 90 100

Ⓑ 80 80 99

Ⓒ 81 91 100

Ⓓ 85 95 100

Directions Have students mark the best answer. **1** Which number tells how many cubes? **2** Count the beads by ones. Which number tells how many? **3** Which set of numbers shows the set of missing numbers in the number chart?

4

1	2	3	4	5	6	7	8	9	10
11	12	13	14	15	16	17	18	19	20
21	22	23	24	25	26	27	28	29	30

Ⓐ 22   Ⓑ 20   Ⓒ 17   Ⓓ 29

✋ 5

51	52	53	54	55	56	57	58	59	60
61	62	63	64	65	66	67	68	69	70
71	72	73	74	75	76	77	78	79	80
81	82	83	84	85	86	87	88	89	90
91	92	93	94	95	96	97	98	99	100

 6

1	2	3	4	5	6	7	8	9	10
11	12	13	14	15	16	17	18	19	20
21	22	23	24	25	26	27	28	29	30
31	32	33	34	35	36	37	38	39	40
41	42	43	44	45	46	47	48	49	50
51	52	53	54	55	56	57	58	59	60
61	62	63	64	65	66	67	68	69	70
71	72	73	74	75	76	77	78	79	80
81	82	83	84	85	86	87	88	89	90
91	92	93	94	95	96	97	98	99	100

🌲 7

11	12	13	14	15		17	18	19	
21		23	24	25	26	27	28	29	
31	32		34	35	36	37	38		
	42	43	44	45	46			49	50
51	52	53	54			57	58	59	60

21   22   28   30

33   35   39   40

41   46   47   48

51   55   56   60

Directions Have students: **4** look at the numbers that are shaded yellow and choose the number that is counted just before the first yellow number. **5** look at the row beginning with 61. Count each number aloud. Have them draw a circle around the part of the number that sounds the same to show the pattern, and then draw a circle around the column that has decade numbers; **6** color the boxes of the numbers as they count by ones, starting at the yellow box and ending at the red box, and then explain any patterns they might see or hear; **7** count by ones to write the missing numbers in the top row, and then draw a circle around each of the missing numbers in the remaining rows.

Topic 11 | Assessment Practice

Name _____

Performance Task

★ 1

1	2	3	4	5	6	7	8	9	10
11	12	13	14	15	16	17	18	●	20
21	22	23	24	25	26	27	28	29	30
31	32	33	34	35	36	37	38	39	40
41	42	43	44	45	46	47	48	49	50

9   19   20

 ❷

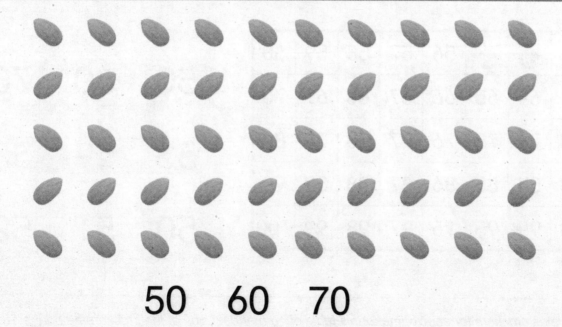

50   60   70

Directions **School Snacks** Say: *It's snack time for the Kindergarten class!* ★ Say: *Keisha puts a grape on the hundred chart to show how many grapes she has in her snack bag.* Have students look at the numbers that come just before and just after the grape, and then at the numbers that are just above and just below it. Have them draw a circle around the missing number that tells how many grapes Keisha has. ❷ Have students count the almonds that Liam and his friends share for their snack. Have them draw a circle around the number that tells how many. If needed, students can use the hundred chart to help.

3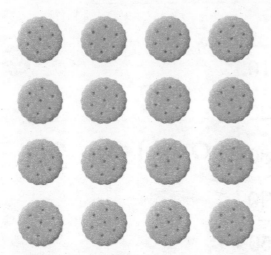

1	2	3	4	5	6	7	8	9	10
11	12	13	14	15	16	17	18	19	20
21	22	23	24	25	26	27	28	29	30

4

5

51	52	🍒	🍒	🍒	56	57	58	59	60
61	62	63	64	65	66	67	68	69	70
71	72	73	74	75	76	77	78	79	80
81	82	83	84	85	86	87	88	89	90
91	92	93	94	95	96	97	98	99	100

50   60   70

53   54   55

50   51   52

Directions **3** Say: *Chen brings crackers for snack time for his table of 10 friends. Look at the crackers he brings.* Have students count the crackers and color that number on the number chart. Say: *How many crackers are left over if each friend has 1 cracker? Color that number on the chart. How do you know you are right?* **4** Say: *Zoe counts the cherries that she gives to her friends. She puts cherries on the number chart for the last three numbers that she counts.* Have students find the cherries in the chart. Then have them look at the numbers to the right of the chart, and then draw a circle around the set of missing numbers to show how Zoe counted the cherries.
5 Say: *Ty has 64 raisins in one bag. He has 18 raisins in another bag. Help Ty count his raisins.* Have students start at 64 on the number chart and make a path to show how to count up 18 in any way they choose. Then have them draw a circle around the number where they stopped, and then explain how they counted up.

 Topic 11 | Performance Task

Identify and Describe Shapes

Essential Question: How can two- and three-dimensional shapes be identified and described?

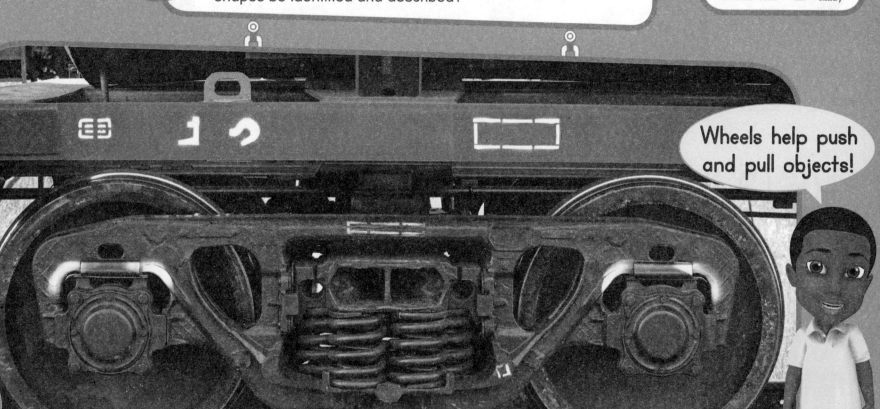

Wheels help push and pull objects!

Wheels

enVision STEM Project: Pushing and Pulling Objects

Directions Read the character speech bubbles to students. **Find Out!** Have students investigate different kinds of wheels. Say: *Not all wheels look alike, but they are all the same shape. Talk to your friends and relatives about the shape of a wheel and ask them how it can help when you need to push and pull objects.* **Journal: Make a Poster** Have students make a poster that shows various objects with wheels. Have them draw up to 5 different kinds of objects that have wheels.

Name _____

Review What You Know

1

10　20　30　40　50

10　12　15　21　30

2

1	2	3	4	5	6	7	8	9	10
11	12	13	14	15	16	17	18	19	20
21	22	23	24	25	26	27	28	29	30
31	32	33	34	35	36	37	38	39	40
41	42	43	44	45	46	47	48	49	50
51	52	53	54	55	56	57	58	59	60
61	62	63	64	65	66	67	68	69	70
71	72	73	74	75	76	77	78	79	80
81	82	83	84	85	86	87	88	89	90
91	92	93	94	95	96	97	98	99	100

3

51	52	53	54	55	56	57	58	59	60
61	62	63	64	65	66	67	68	69	70
71	72	73	74	75	76	77	78	79	80
81	82	83	84	85	86	87	88	89	90
91	92	93	94	95	96	97	98	99	100

4

_ _ _ _ _ _ _ _ _ _

5

_ _ _ _ _ _ _ _ _

6

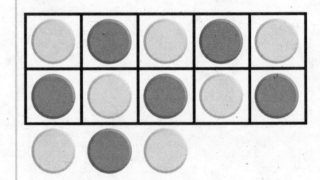

23　　8　　13

Directions Have students: **1** draw a circle around the set of numbers that shows a pattern of counting by tens; **2** draw a circle around the hundred chart; **3** draw a circle around the numbers *fifty-five* and *ninety-nine*; **4** count the objects, write the numbers, and then draw a circle around the number that is greater than the other number; **5** count the objects, and then write the number; **6** draw a circle around the number that tells how many counters.

Name _____

A

B

Directions Say: *You will choose one of these projects. Look at picture* **A.** *Think about this question: Where did all those bones come from? If you choose Project A, you will create dinosaur puzzles. Look at picture* **B.** *Think about this question: Would you rather design buildings or build them? If you choose Project B, you will design and build a structure.*

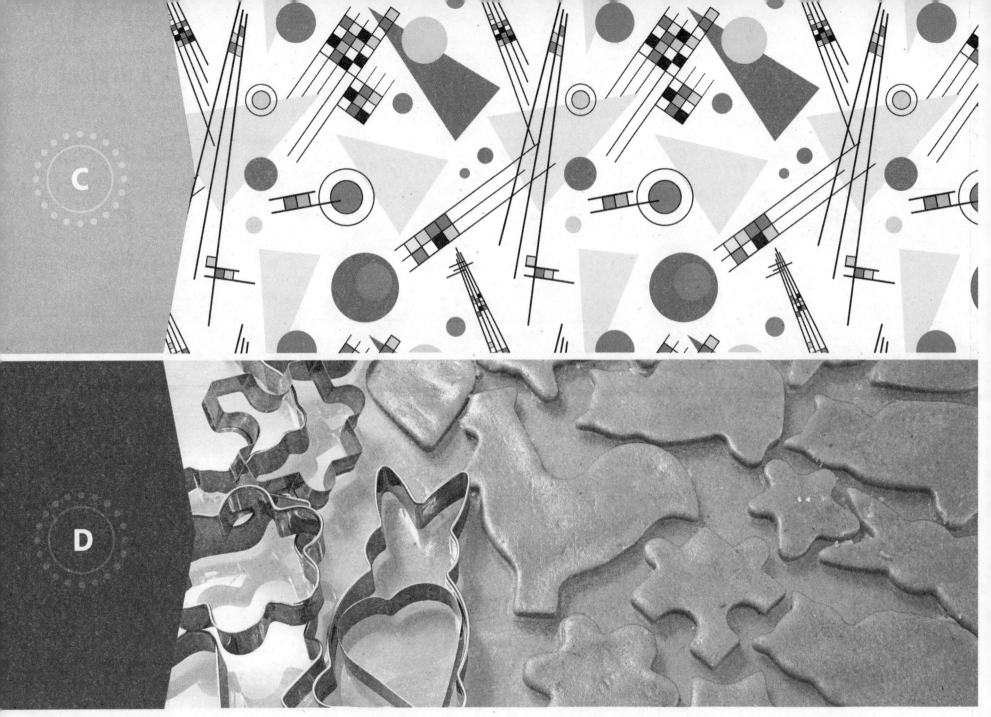

Directions Say: *You will choose one of these projects. Look at picture C. Think about this question: What can you draw using only triangles? If you choose Project C, you will make a shape picture. Look at picture D. Think about this question: How are all those cookies made? If you choose Project D, you will act out a party.*

Name _____

Activity

Directions Say: *Pick 6 shapes from a bag. Put the shapes into two groups. Tell how the groups are different. Then draw a picture of the shapes you put on each table.*

I can ...
name shapes as flat or solid.

Content Standards K.G.A.3 Also K.CC.A.1, K.MD.2.3 **Mathematical Practices** MP.3, MP.6, and MP.7

flat

solid

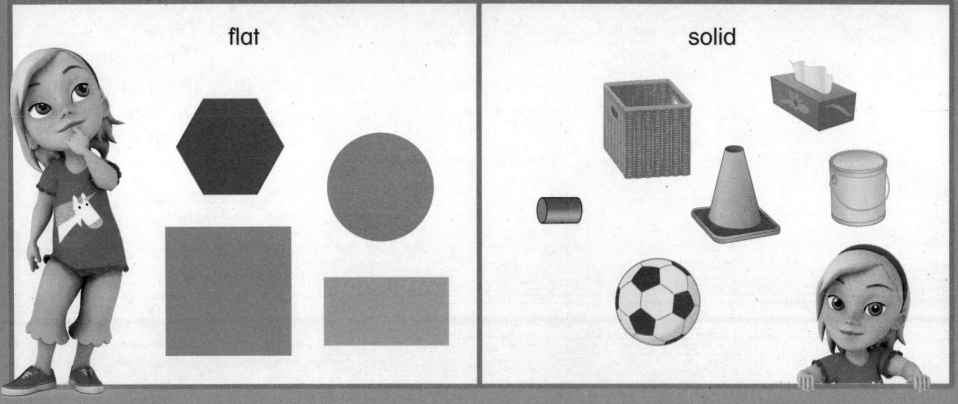

☆ **Guided Practice**

1

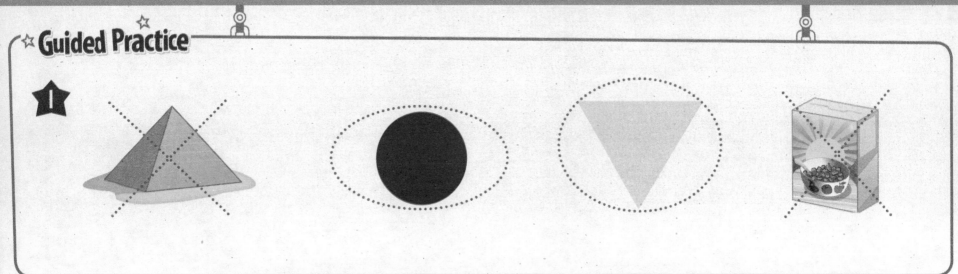

Directions ⭐ Have students draw a circle around the objects that are flat, and mark an X on the objects that are solid.

Topic 12 | Lesson 1

Name _____

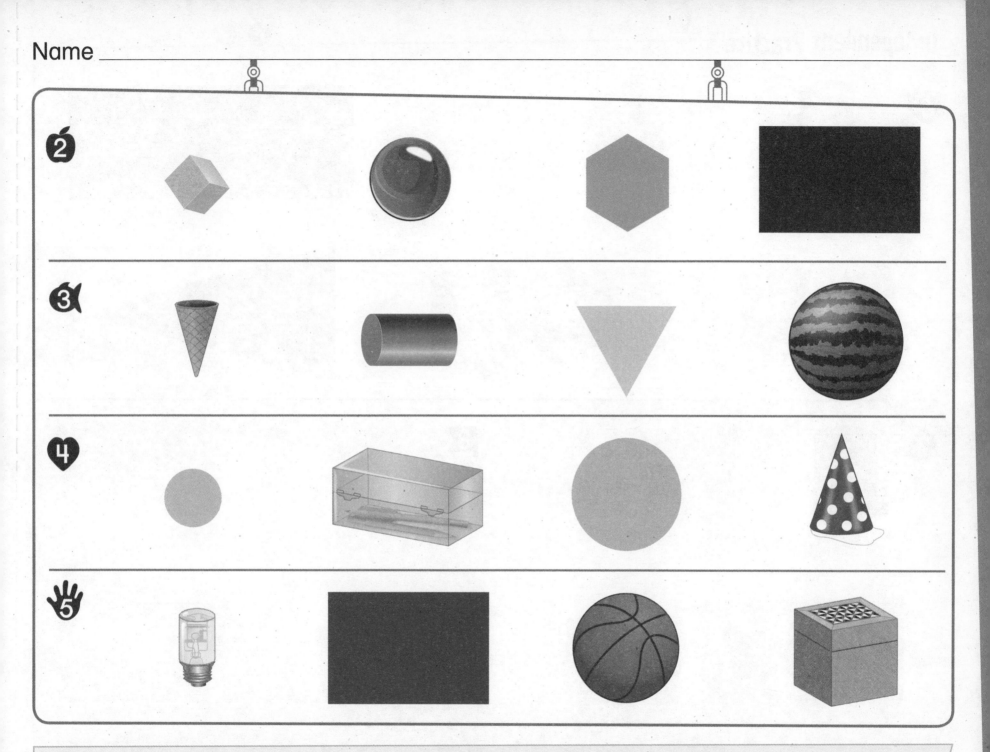

2 🍎

3 🐟

4 ❤️

5 ✋

Directions Have students: **2** and **3** draw a circle around the objects that are flat in each row, and then mark an X on the objects that are solid; **4** mark an X on the objects that are NOT flat; **5** mark an X on the objects that are NOT solid.

Topic 12 | Lesson 1   four hundred sixty-seven **467**

Independent Practice

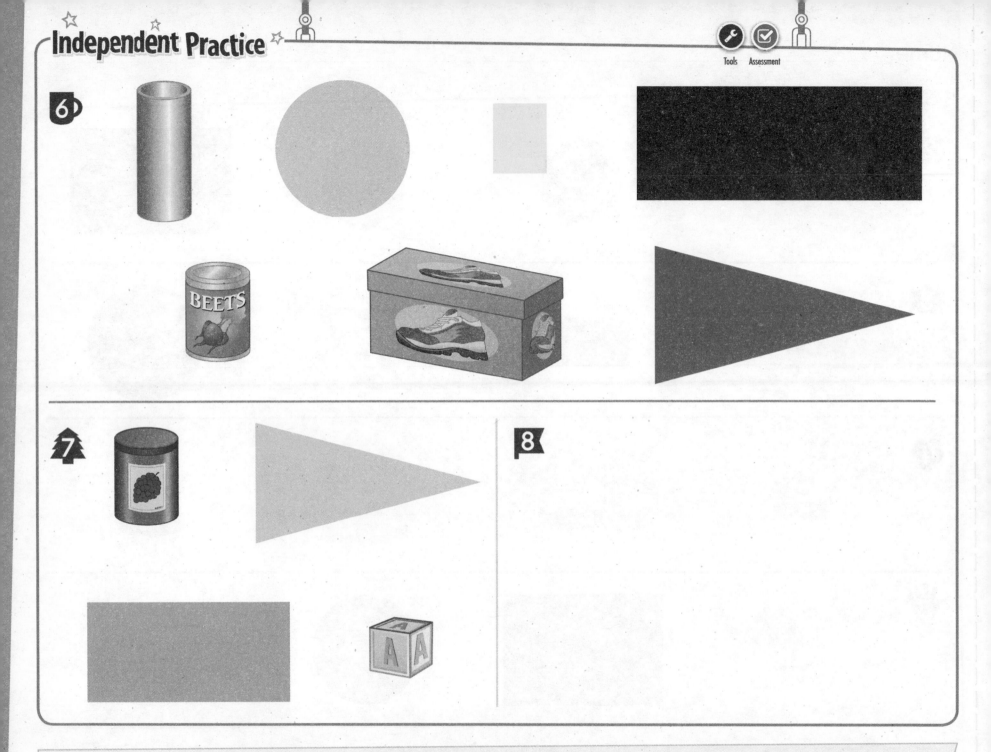

6

7

8

Directions Have students: **6** mark an X on the objects that are solid. Then have them draw a circle around the objects that are flat; **7** mark an X on the objects that are NOT solid. **8** **Higher Order Thinking** Have students draw a picture of an object that is solid.

468 four hundred sixty-eight   Copyright © SAVVAS Learning Company LLC. All Rights Reserved.   **Topic 12** | Lesson 1

Name _____

Activity

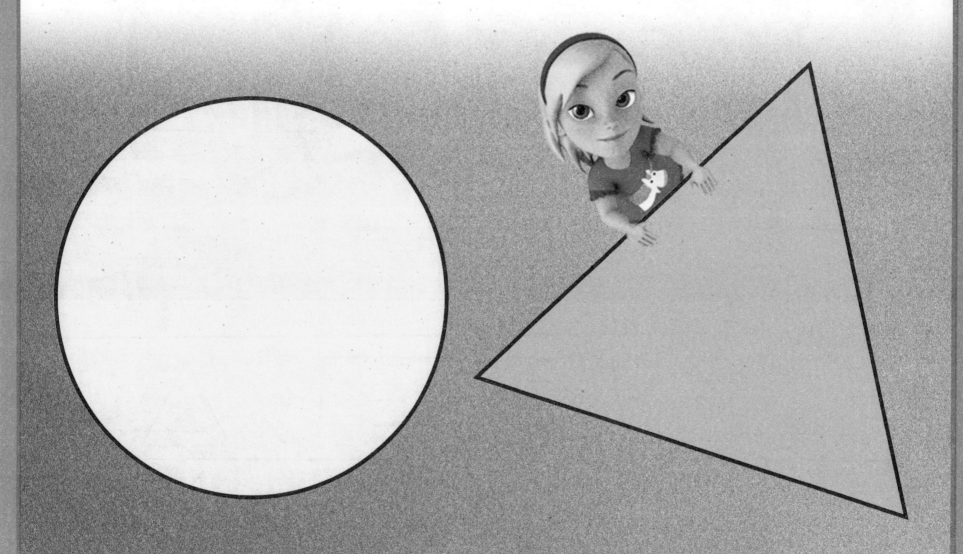

Directions Say: *Go on a shape hunt. Find shapes and objects in the classroom or outside that look like the shapes shown on the page. Draw the shapes. Use your own words to tell where you found them. Then say:* Tell how the shapes are different.

I can ...
identify and describe circles and triangles.

 Content Standards K.G.A.2 Also K.CC.A.1, K.G.A.1 **Mathematical Practices** MP.2, MP.6, and MP.7

☆ **Guided Practice**

1

2

Directions 1 and 2 Have students color the circle in each row, and then mark an X on each triangle.

Name _____

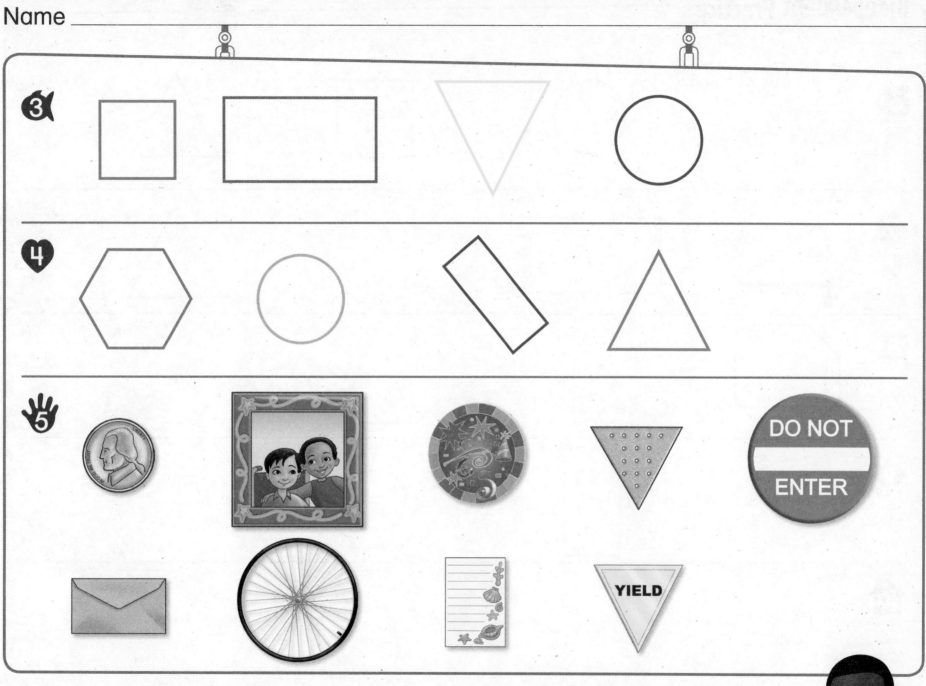

3

4

5

DO NOT ENTER

YIELD

Directions **3** Have students color the circle and mark an X on the triangle. **4** **Number Sense** Have students mark an X on the shape that has 3 sides. **5** Have students mark an X on the objects that look like a triangle, and then draw a box around the objects that look like a circle.

Independent Practice

Tools Assessment

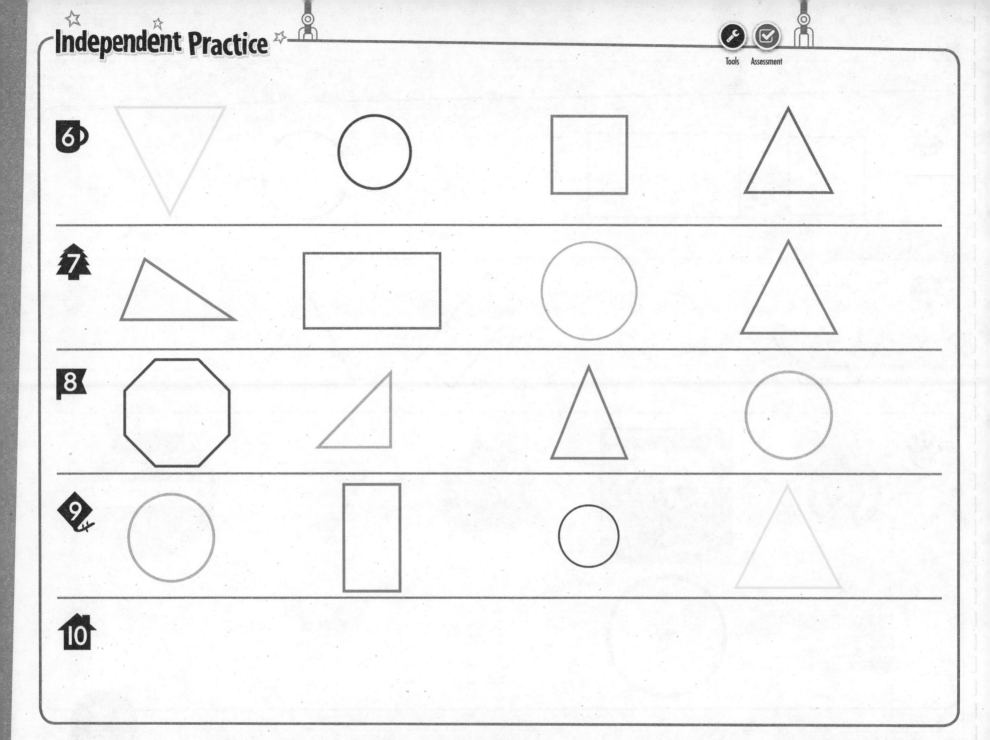

6

7

8

9

10

Directions **6**–**9** Have students color the circles and mark an X on the triangles in each row. **10** **Higher Order Thinking** Have students draw a picture of an object that is shaped like a triangle.

472 four hundred seventy-two

Topic 12 | Lesson 2

 Solve & Share

Name _____

Activity

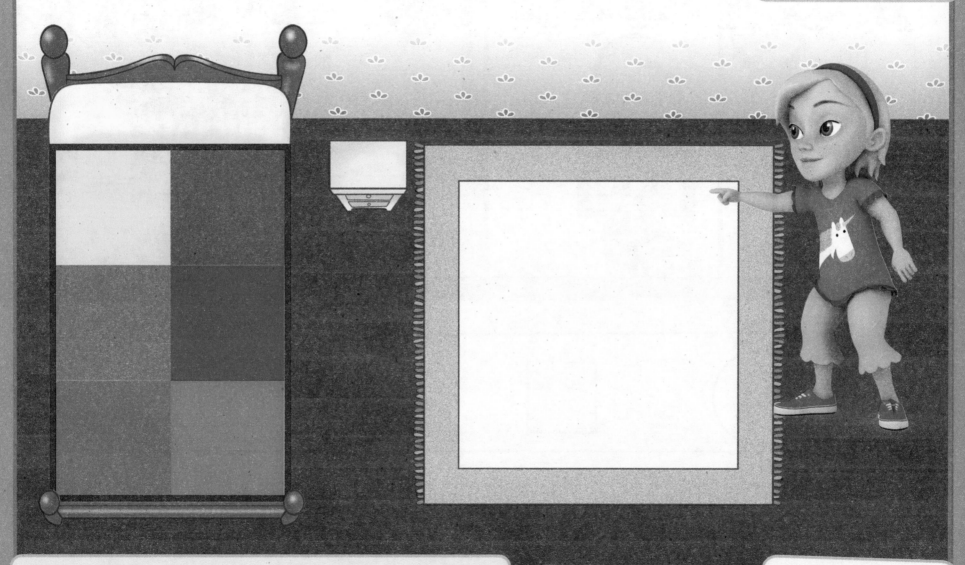

Directions Say: *Emily has a large quilt on her bed. The shape outlined with black lines is a rectangle. The rectangular quilt is made up of square rectangles of different colors. How many other rectangles can you find in the picture? How many of the rectangles are squares? Count the shapes and tell where you see them.*

I can ...
identify and describe squares and other rectangles.

© **Content Standards** K.G.A.2 Also K.CC.A.1, K.G.A.1, K.G.B.4 **Mathematical Practices** MP.6, MP.7, and MP.8

☆ **Guided Practice**

⭐ 1

2

Directions ⭐ and ❷ Have students color the rectangles in each row, and then mark an X on each rectangle that is also a square.

474 four hundred seventy-four   Copyright © SAVVAS Learning Company LLC. All Rights Reserved.   **Topic 12** | Lesson 3

Name _____

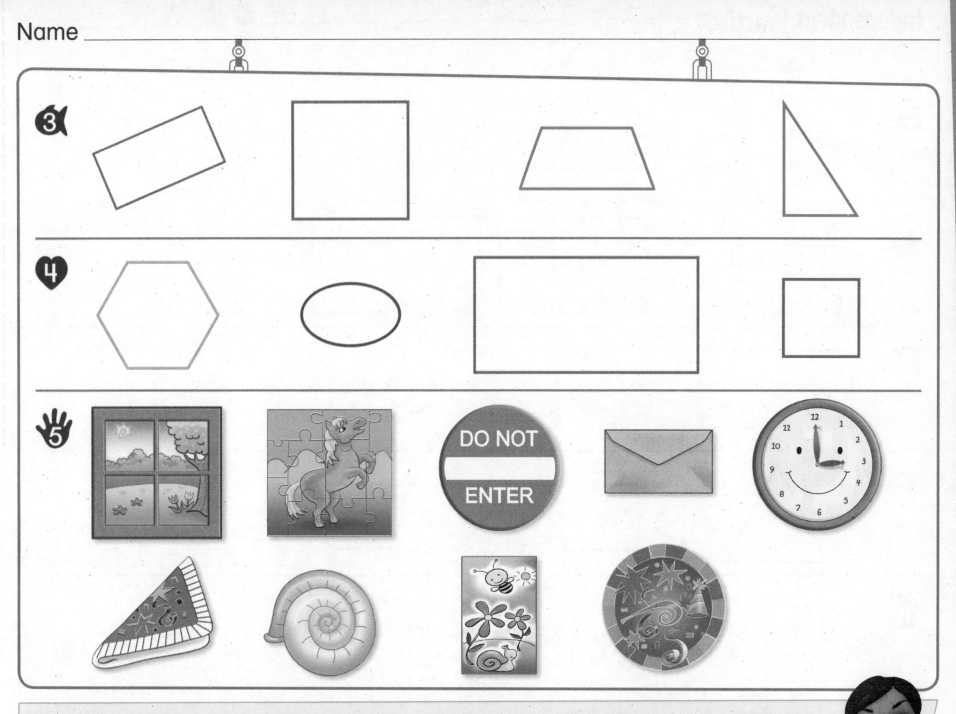

3

4

5

DO NOT ENTER

Directions Have students: **3** and **4** color the rectangles in each row, and then mark an X on each rectangle that is also a square; **5** draw a circle around the objects that look like a rectangle, and then mark an X on each object that also looks like a square. Have students tell how they know which objects to mark with an X. Say: *How are rectangles and squares the same? How are they different?*

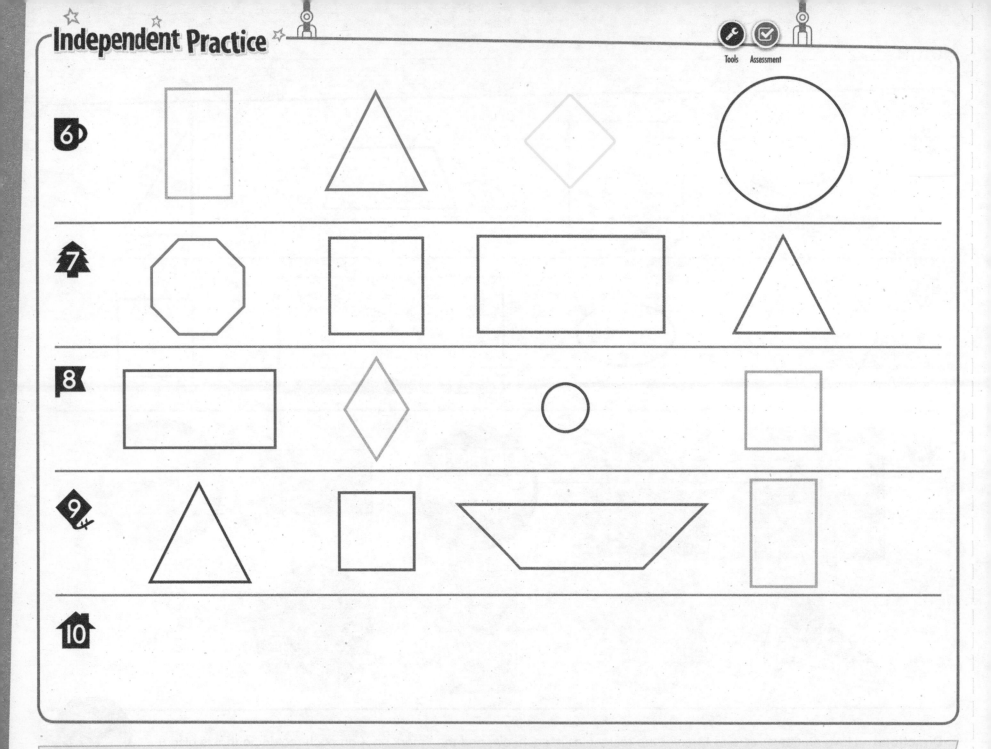

6

7

8

9

10

Directions **6**–**9** Have students color the rectangles in each row, and then mark an X on each rectangle that is also a square.
10 Higher Order Thinking Have students draw a green rectangle, and then draw a yellow square.

476 four hundred seventy-six   Copyright © SAVVAS Learning Company LLC. All Rights Reserved.   **Topic 12** | Lesson 3

Name _____

I can ...
describe and identify
hexagons.

© **Content Standards** K.G.A.2
Also K.CC.A.1, K.G.A.1, K.G.B.4
Mathematical Practices MP.5,
MP.6, and MP.7

Directions Say: *Emily wants to buy art that has six-sided shapes in it like the yellow pattern block. Draw a circle around all the pieces of art that she can buy.*

☆ **Guided Practice**

⭐ 1

🍎 2

Directions ⭐ and 🍎 Have students color the hexagon in each row.

Topic 12 | Lesson 4

Name _____

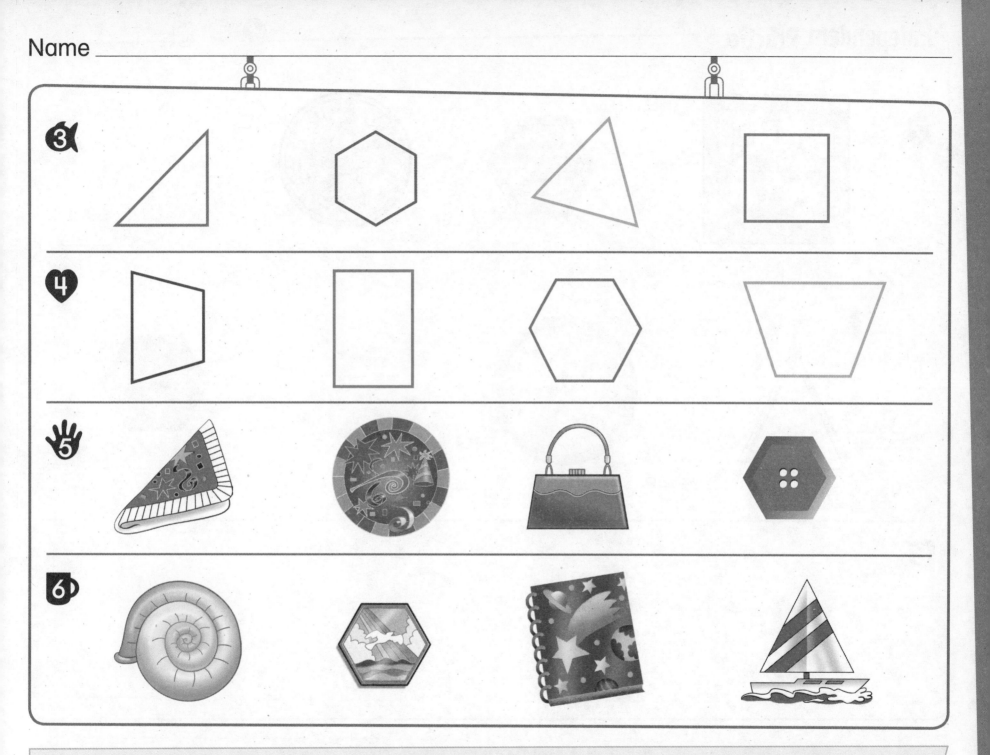

Directions Have students: ❸ and ❹ color the hexagon; ✋ and ❻ draw a circle around the object that looks like a hexagon. Then have students tell how they decided which object to circle.

Independent Practice

 7

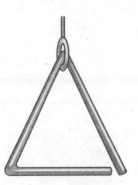   

8

Directions ✿ Have students draw a circle around the objects that look like a hexagon. **8 Higher Order Thinking** Have students draw a picture using at least 1 hexagon.

 Topic 12 | Lesson 4

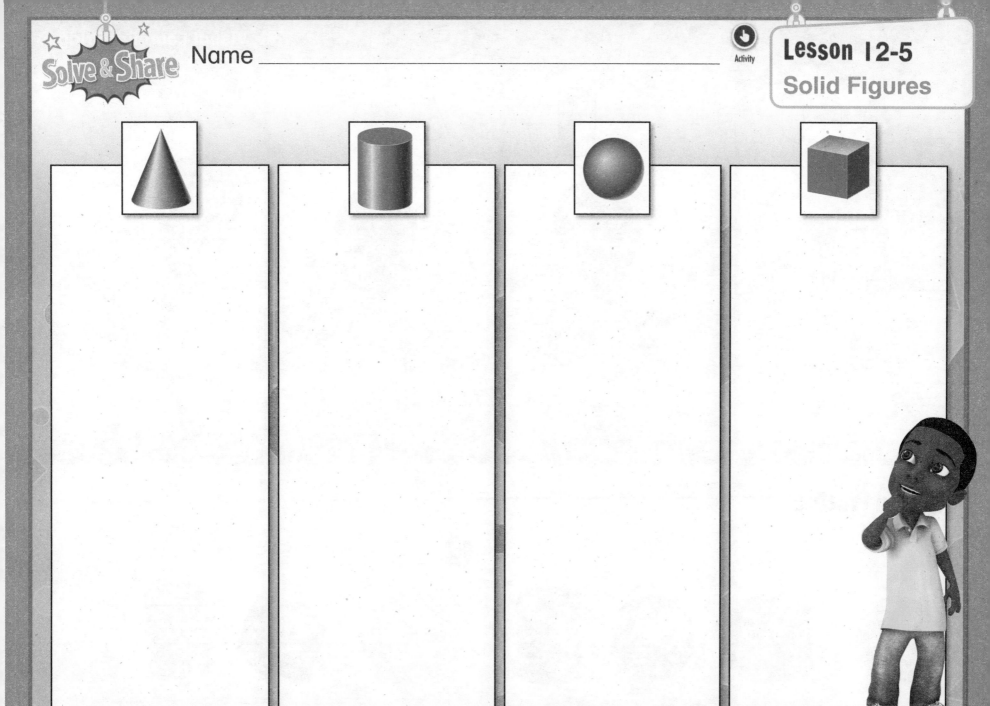

Directions Say: *Jackson wants to find objects that have the same shape as the solid figures. How can he find objects that have the same shape? Draw objects below each solid figure that have the same shape.*

I can ...
describe and identify solid figures.

© **Content Standards** K.G.A.2 Also K.G.A.1, K.G.B.4
Mathematical Practices MP.2, MP.4, and MP.7

☆ Guided Practice

1

2

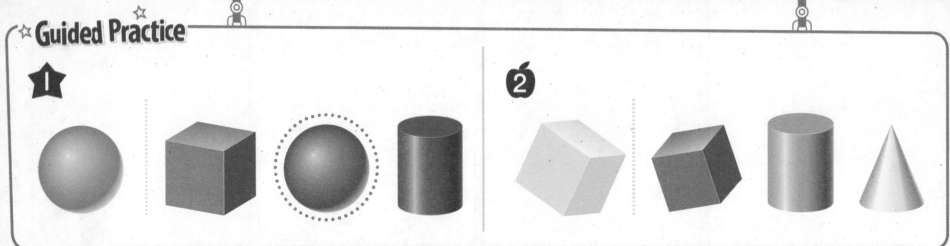

Directions 🌟 and 🍎 Have students name the solid figure on the left, and then draw a circle around the solid figure on the right that is the same shape.

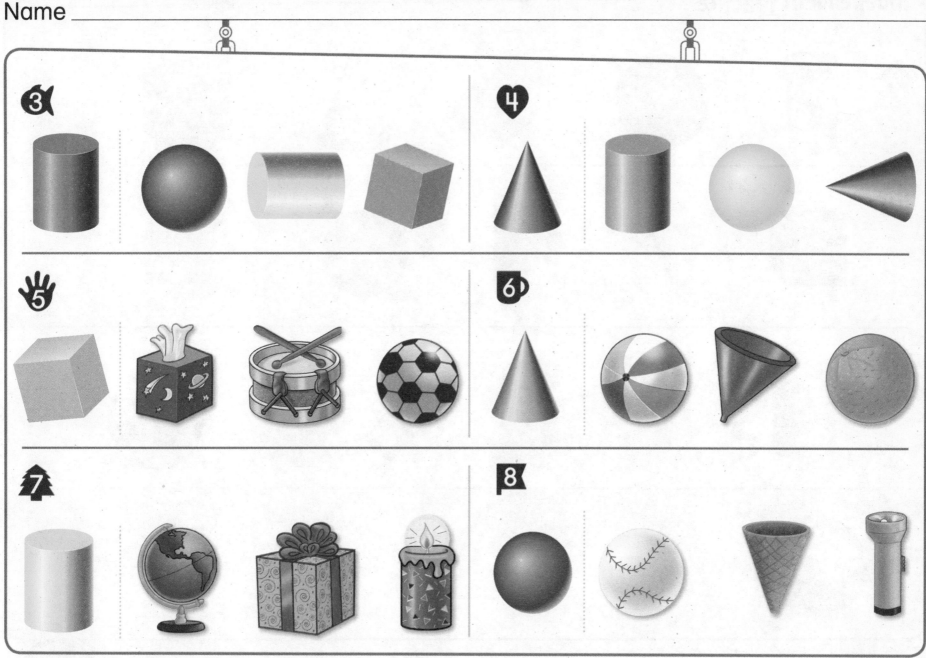

Directions 3 and 4 Have students name the solid figure on the left, and then draw a circle around the solid figure on the right that is the same shape. 5–8 Have students name the solid figure on the left, and then draw a circle around the object on the right that looks like that shape. Then have students see if they can find objects in the classroom that look like a cone, a cylinder, or a sphere.

Independent Practice

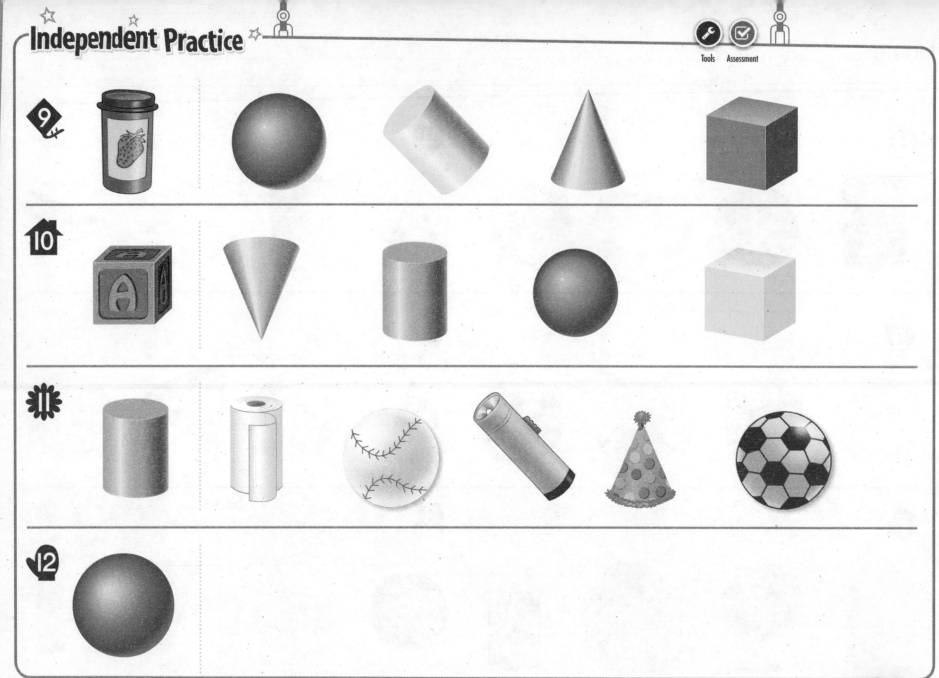

9

10

11

12

Directions Have students: **9** and **10** look at the object on the left, and then draw a circle around the solid figure on the right that looks like that shape; **11** name the solid figure on the left, and then draw a circle around the objects on the right that look like that shape. **12 Higher Order Thinking** Have students name the solid figure on the left, and then draw 2 more objects that look like that shape.

Topic 12 | Lesson 5

Solve & Share

Activity

Lesson 12-6

Describe
Shapes in the
Environment

Name _____

Directions Say: *Draw a circle around two of the shapes on the workmat. Name the shapes. Can you find the shapes you circled in your classroom? Use your own words to tell where you found them. Draw a picture of the objects and their surroundings.*

I can ...
describe shapes in the environment.

© **Content Standards** K.G.A.1
Also K.G.A.2, K.G.A.3
Mathematical Practices MP.1, MP.3, and MP.6

☆ Guided Practice

★1

Directions ★ Have students mark an X on the object next to the pencil that looks like a rectangle. Have students draw an object that looks like a square in front of the mug. Then have them draw an object that looks like a cone next to the table.

Name _____

Directions ❷ **Vocabulary** Have students name the shape of the objects in the picture and use position words to describe their location. Then have them draw an X on the object in front of the sand castle that looks like a **cylinder**. Have students draw an object that looks like a **sphere** beside Jackson, and then an object that looks like a **rectangle** next to the sandbox.

Independent Practice

3

4

Directions ❸ Have students point to objects in the picture and name each shape. Then have them draw a circle around the objects that look like a cylinder, and mark an X on the objects that look like a cone. ❹ **Higher Order Thinking** Have students: mark an X on the object below the tree that looks like a rectangle; draw an object that looks like a circle above the tree; and draw an object that looks like a triangle behind the fence. Then have them name the shape of objects in the picture and use position words to describe their locations.

Topic 12 | Lesson 6

Solve & Share

Think.

Directions Say: *Emily's teacher teaches her class a game. She uses I blue cube, I red cube, I yellow counter, and I red counter and puts each of them somewhere on the farm picture. Play this game with a partner. Place the tools on the page, and then describe where one of them is located. Do NOT tell your partner which one you are talking about. How can your partner tell which one you are describing? Change places and play again.*

I can ...
describe positions of shapes in the environment.

© **Mathematical Practices** MP.6
Also MP.2, MP.3
Content Standards K.G.A.1
Also K.G.A.2

Go Online | SavvasRealize.com

☆ Guided Practice

1

Directions **1** Have students mark an X on the object above the bed that looks like a cube. Then have them explain how they know they are correct. Then have them draw a shape that looks like a rectangle next to the bed.

Name _____

Tools   Assessment

Independent Practice

2

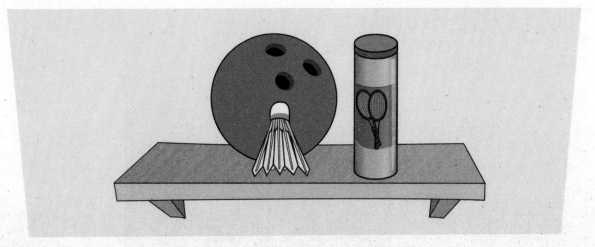

3

Directions **2** Have students name the shapes of the objects in the picture. Then have them mark an X on the object that is behind another object, and is next to the object that looks like a cylinder. Have them explain how they decided which shape to mark. **3** Have students find the object in the picture that is NOT beside the box of tissues, and then mark an X on the solid it looks like on the left. Have them explain why a sphere is NOT the right answer. Then have them name the shapes of the objects in the picture.

Directions Read the problem to students. Then have them use multiple problem-solving methods to solve the problem. Say: *Carlos wants to tell a friend about different things in the locker room and where they are located. What words can he use?* ❹ **Be Precise** *Mark an X on the object that looks like a cylinder that is beside the object that looks like a cube. What words helped you find the correct object?* ✋ **Reason** *Carlos says the soccer ball is behind the water bottle. What is another way to explain where the water bottle is?* ❻ **Explain** *Carlos describes the rectangle poster as being above the circle clock. Do you agree or disagree? Explain how you know you are correct.*

⭐ 1

5 − 2	3 − 1	1 − 1	2 + 0	5 − 4
5 − 0	0 + 2	3 + 1	2 − 0	1 + 2
1 + 4	2 + 0	4 − 2	5 − 3	4 − 0
0 + 1	1 + 1	4 − 3	3 − 1	4 − 1
3 + 2	4 − 2	0 + 3	1 + 1	4 − 4

🍎 2

_____

— — — — —

_____

Directions Have students: ⭐ color each box that has a sum or difference that is equal to 2; 🍎 write the letter that they see.

I can ...
add and subtract fluently within 5.

© **Content Standard** K.OA.A.5
Mathematical Practices MP.3, MP.6, MP.7, and MP.8

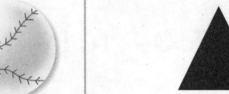

Directions **Understand Vocabulary** Have students: ⭐ draw a circle around the **two-dimensional** shape; 🍎 draw a circle around the **three-dimensional** shape; 🦋 draw a circle around the **vertices** of the triangle; ❤️ draw a **circle**; ✋ draw a shape that is NOT a **square**.

Name ______________________________

TOPIC 12

Reteaching

Set A

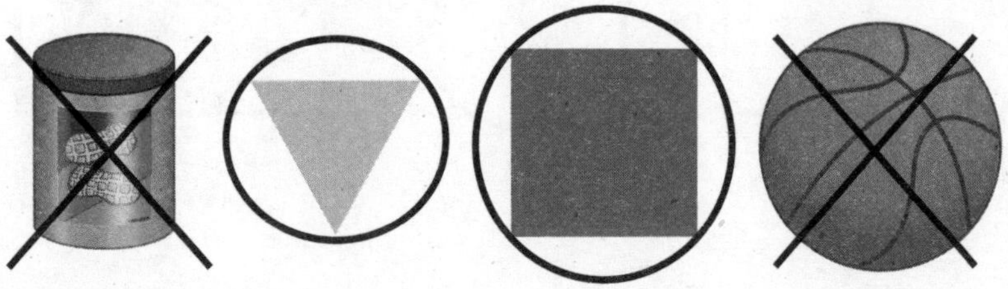

1

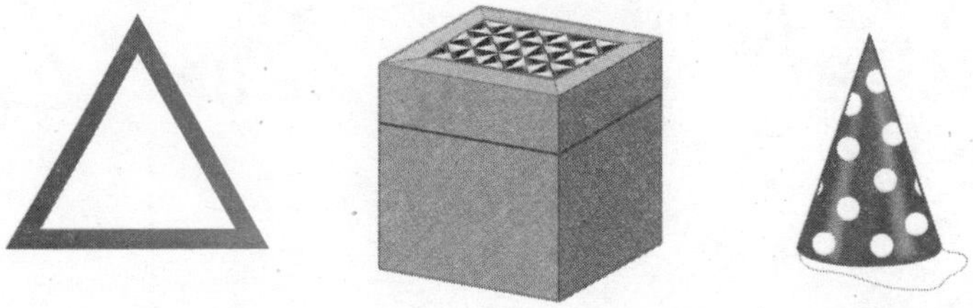

Set B

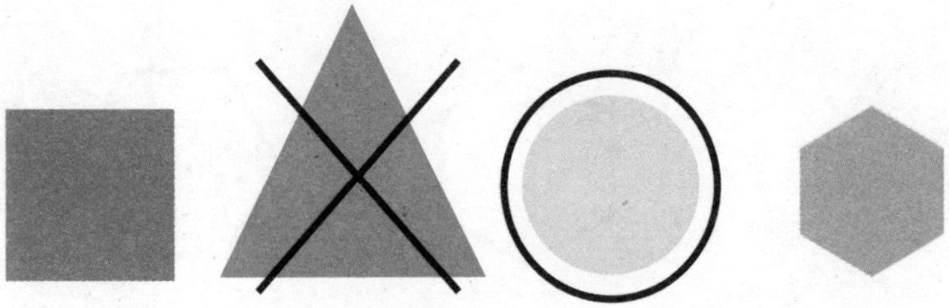

2

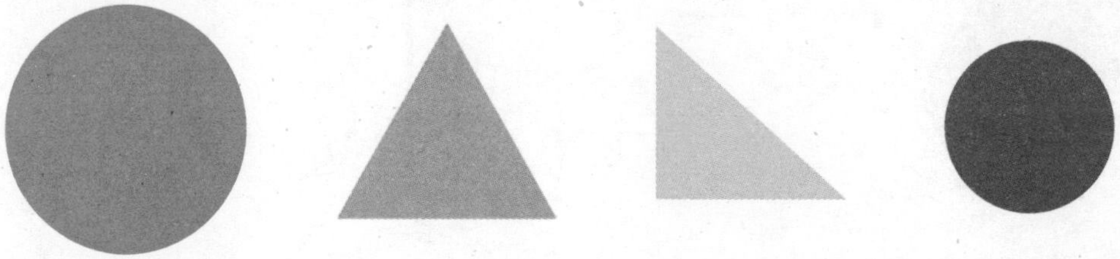

Directions Have students: 1 draw a circle around the objects that are flat, and then mark an X on the objects that are solid; 2 draw a circle around the objects that look like a circle, and then mark an X on the objects that look like a triangle.

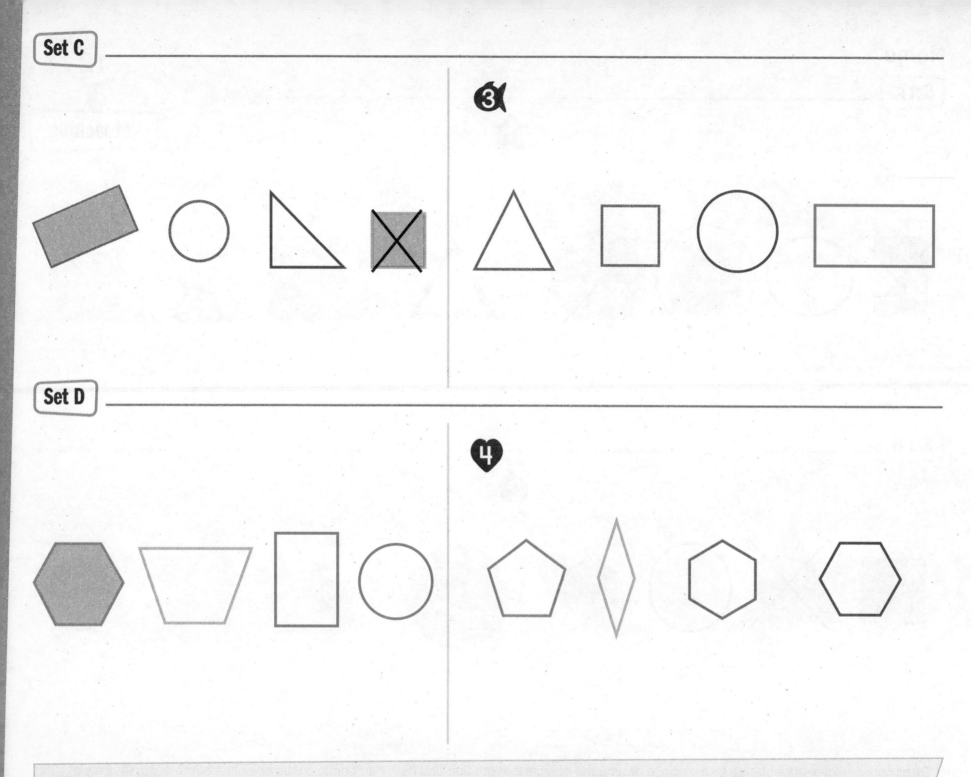

Directions Have students: ③ color the rectangles, and then mark an X on the rectangle that is a square; ④ color the hexagons.

Topic 12 | Reteaching

Name _____

_____

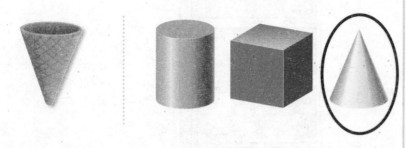

Set F

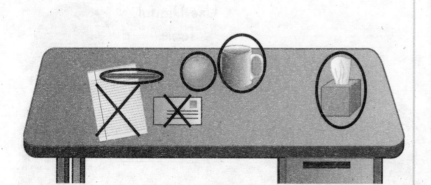

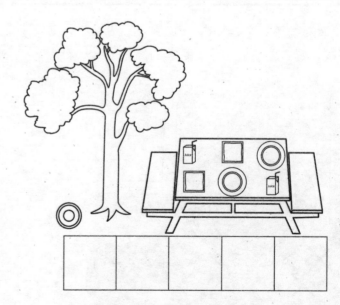

Directions Have students: 🖐 name the solid figure on the left, and then draw a circle around the solid figure that looks like that shape on the right; 🔢 point to each object in the picture and tell what shape each looks like. Then have them draw a circle around the objects that are solid, and mark an X on objects that are flat.

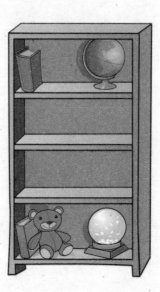

Set G

Use Digital Tools.

Directions Have students: **7** mark an X on the object that is next to the blue book, and then draw a circle around the object that is below the object that is shaped like a sphere; **8** mark an X on the objects that look like a circle that are behind the object that is shaped like a sphere.

Topic 12 | Reteaching

Name _____

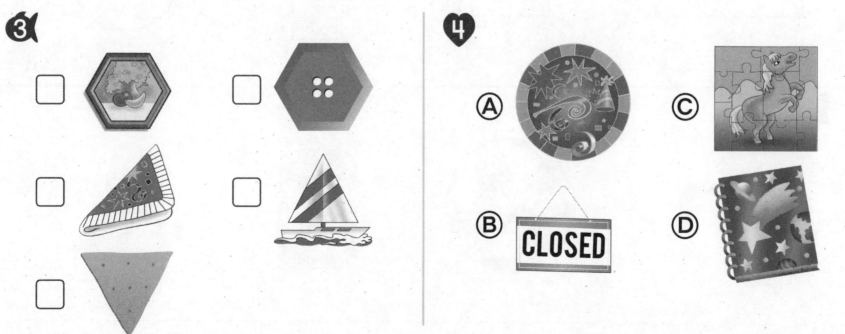

⭐ 1

Ⓐ

Ⓒ

Ⓑ

Ⓓ

🍎 2

Ⓐ

Ⓒ

Ⓑ

Ⓓ

3

☐ ☐

☐ ☐

☐

4

Ⓐ

Ⓒ

Ⓑ CLOSED

Ⓓ

Directions Have students mark the best answer. ⭐ Which object is NOT solid? 🍎 Which object is NOT a triangle? 3 Choose two objects that look like a hexagon. 4 Which object looks like a square?

Topic 12 | Assessment Practice

four hundred ninety-nine **499**

5

 6

 7

Directions Have students: mark an X on the objects that do NOT look like a circle; name the shapes, color the rectangles, and then mark an X on the rectangle that is a square; look at the solid figure on the left, and then draw a circle around the object that looks like that shape.

Topic 12 | Assessment Practice

Name _____

8

9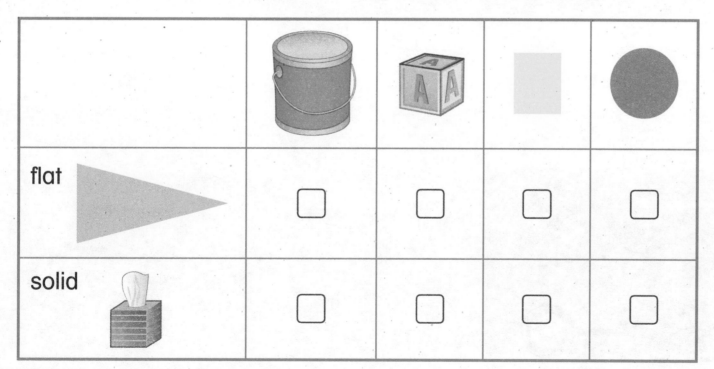

flat	☐	☐	☐	☐
solid	☐	☐	☐	☐

Directions Have students: 8 draw an object that looks like a cylinder in front of the vase. Then mark an X on the object that looks like a square next to the cat; 9 choose *flat* or *solid* for each image.

Directions Have students: draw a picture of an object that looks like a sphere below a book and next to a cup; draw a picture of an object that is flat. Then have them draw an object that is solid; draw a circle around the objects that look like a circle, and then mark an X on the objects that look like a rectangle.

Name _____

TOPIC 12

Performance Task

⭐ 1

🍎 2

Directions **Play Time!** Say: *Supna and her friends are playing with toys.* Have students: ⭐ draw a circle around the toys that look like a cube. Have students mark an X on the toys that look like a cylinder; 🍎 draw a circle around the toys that look like a rectangle. Then have them mark an X on the rectangles that are squares.

Topic 12 | Performance Task

five hundred three **503**

Directions Have students: ➌ mark an X on the object in the playroom that looks like a hexagon; ➍ draw an object next to the shelves that looks like a cone; ✋ listen to the clues, and then draw a circle around the object the clues describe. Say: *The object is above the blocks. It looks like a sphere. It is next to a green ball. The object is NOT yellow.*

Topic 12 | Performance Task

Analyze, Compare, and Create Shapes

Essential Question: How can solid figures be named, described, compared, and composed?

Digital Resources

Interactive Student Edition · Activity · Visual Learning · Video · Practice

Assessment · Games · Tools · Glossary

ēnVision STEM Project: How Do Objects Move?

Directions Read the character speech bubbles to students. **Find Out!** Have students observe and describe how objects move using the terms *roll*, *stack*, and *slide*. Say: *Objects move in different ways. Talk to your friends and relatives about everyday objects that are cones, cylinders, spheres, or cubes. Ask them how each one moves and whether they roll, stack, or slide.* **Journal: Make a Poster** Have students make a poster that shows everyday objects that are cones, cylinders, spheres, and cubes, and then tell how each one moves.

Name _____

Review What You Know

1

○ □ △

2

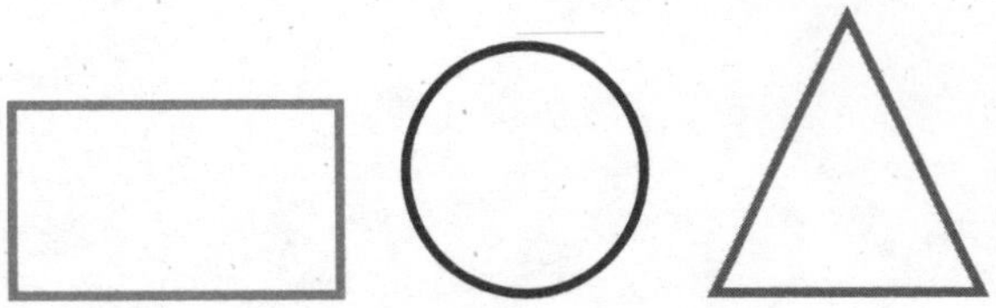

▭ ○ △

3

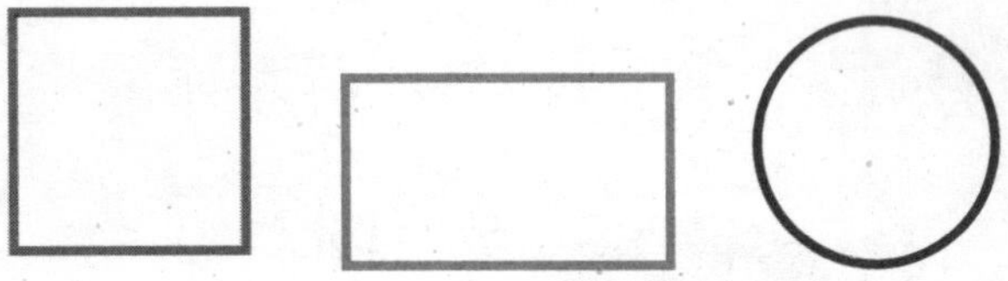

□ ▭ ○

4

▶ ■
▲ ♥

5

■ ■
▲ ●

6

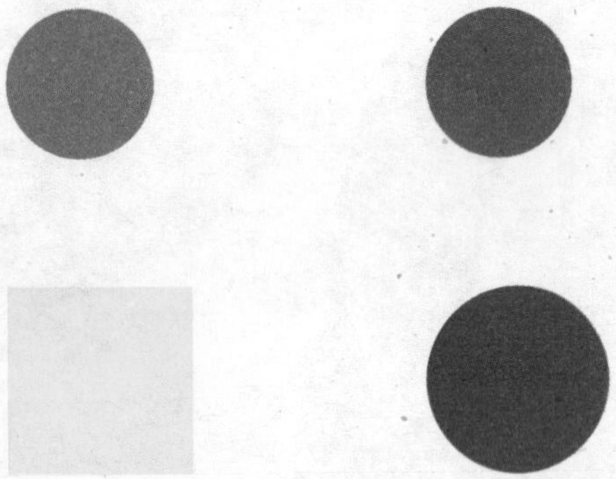

● ●
■ ●

Name _____

A

B

C

Directions Say: *You will choose one of these projects. Look at picture* **A.** *Think about this question: Have you eaten any circles or squares lately? If you choose Project A, you will make a kitchen shapes poster. Look at picture* **B.** *Think about this question: Do you enjoy puppet shows? If you choose Project B, you will create a puppet show. Look at picture* **C.** *Think about this question: How would you describe the shapes in this quilt? If you choose Project C, you will design a patchwork quilt.*

Math Modeling

Pieced Together

Video

> What can I make?

Directions Read the robot's speech bubble to students. **Generate Interest** Ask students about their experience with shapes. Say: *Can you use smaller rectangles to make a larger one? Can you use triangles to make a rectangle?* Give students a chance to practice making shapes out of smaller shapes.

I can ...
model with math using 2-D shapes to solve a problem.

© **Mathematical Practices** MP.4
Also MP.3, MP.5
Content Standards K.G.B.6
Also K.G.A.1, K.G.A.2

Solve & Share

Name _____

Activity

Directions Say: *Emily wants to figure out which shapes are behind the door. The mystery shapes that are behind the door have only 4 vertices (corners). Use the shapes shown above the door to help you decide which shapes are behind the door. Draw the shapes that match the clue on the door. How many shapes did you draw? Write that number next to the door. Now mark an X on the shapes that are NOT behind the door. Count those shapes and write the number. Look at the two numbers you wrote. Circle the number that is greater than the other number. If the numbers are the same, circle both numbers. Name the shapes that are behind the door.*

I can ...
analyze and compare 2-D shapes.

© **Content Standards** K.G.B.4 Also K.CC.C.6
Mathematical Practices MP.4, MP.6, and MP.7

☆ **Guided Practice**

1

2

Directions Have students listen to the clues, mark an X on the shapes that do NOT fit the clues, draw a circle around the shape that the clues describe, and then tell how the shapes they marked with an X are different from the shape they drew a circle around. ⭐ *I have 4 sides. I do NOT have 4 sides that are the same length. What shape am I?* ❷ *I do NOT have 4 sides. I do NOT have any vertices. What shape am I?*

510 five hundred ten

Topic 13 | Lesson I

Name _____

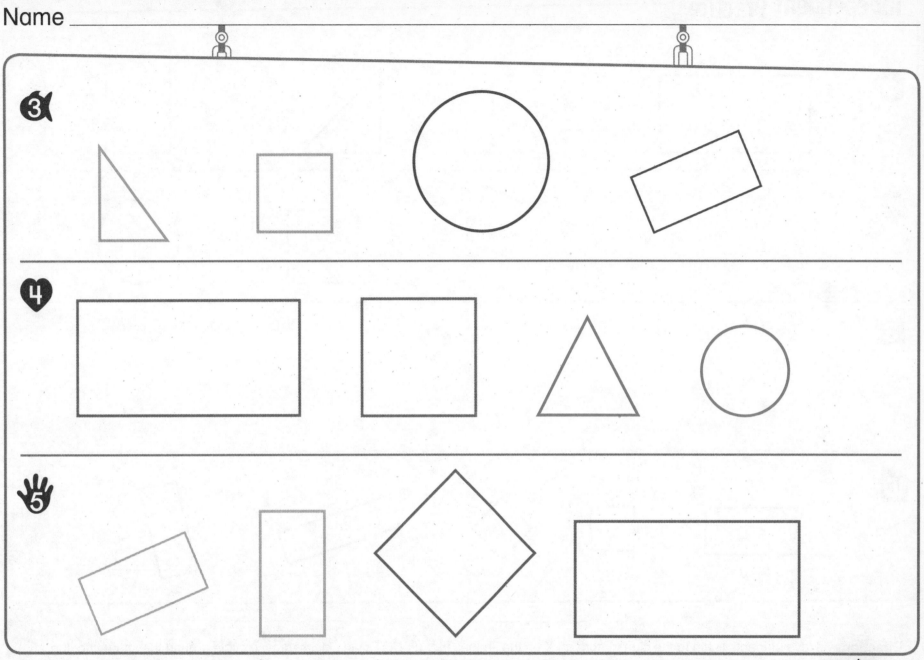

❸

❤

✋5

Directions Have students listen to the clues, mark an X on the shapes that do NOT fit the clues, draw a circle around the shape that the clues describe, and then tell how the shapes they marked with an X are similar to the shape they drew a circle around.
❸ **Number Sense** *I am NOT round. I have less than 4 sides. What shape am I?* ❤ *I am NOT a rectangle. I have 0 sides. What shape am I?* ✋5 *I have 4 vertices. I am a special kind of rectangle because all my sides are the same length. What shape am I?*

Independent Practice

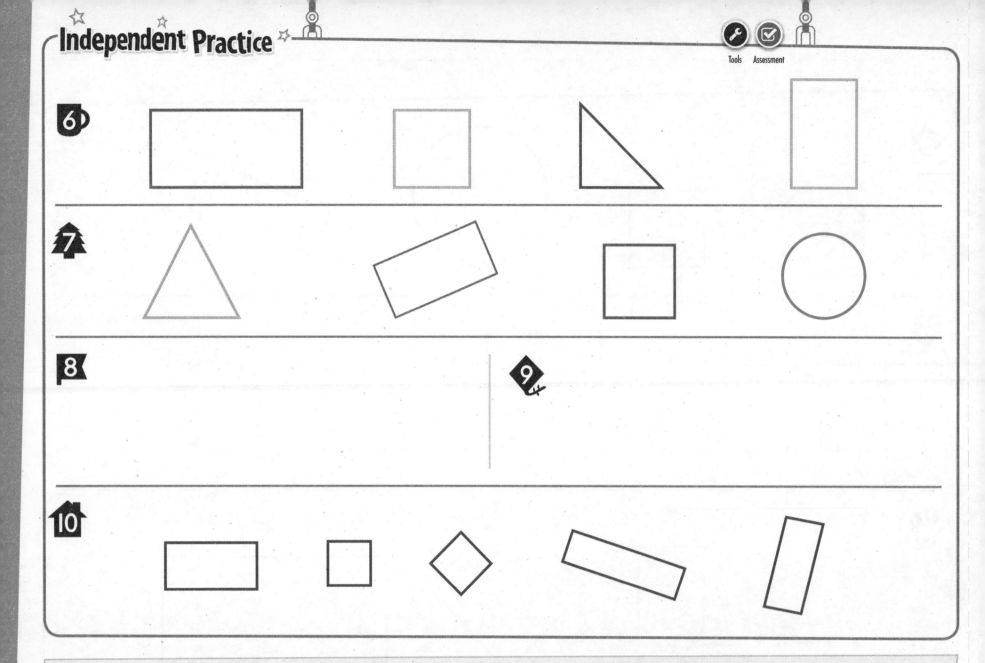

6

7

8

9

10

Tools   Assessment

Directions Have students listen to the clues, mark an X on the shapes that do NOT fit the clues, draw a circle around the shape that the clues describe, and then tell how the shapes they marked with an X are different from the shape they drew a circle around. **6** *All of my sides are NOT the same length. I have 3 vertices. What shape am I?* **7** *I have 4 sides. I am the same shape as a classroom door. What shape am I?* **8** Have students listen to the clues, and then draw the shape the clues describe: *I have more than 3 sides. The number of vertices I have is less than 5. All of my sides are the same length. What shape am I?* **9 Higher Order Thinking** Have students draw a shape with 4 sides and 4 vertices that is NOT a square or rectangle, and then explain why it is not. **10 Higher Order Thinking** Have students draw a circle around the rectangles. Have them color all the squares, and then explain how the shapes are both similar and different from one another.

       Topic 13 | Lesson 1

Activity

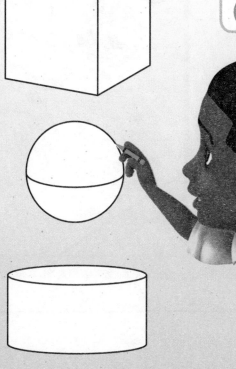

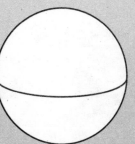

Directions Say: *Jackson wants to find a solid figure. The solid figure has more than one flat side and it rolls. Color the solid figures that match the description. Then count them. How many are there? How many shapes do you see in all?*

I can ...
analyze and compare 3-D shapes.

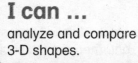

Content Standards K.G.B.4 Also K.CC.B.5, K.G.B.5
Mathematical Practices MP.2, MP.3, and MP.7

☆ Guided Practice

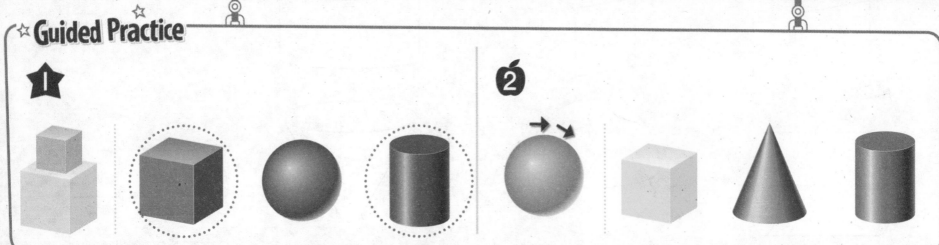

1

2

Directions Have students: **1** look at the stacked solid figures on the left, and then draw a circle around the other solid figures that stack; **2** look at the rolling solid figure on the left, and then draw a circle around the other solid figures that roll.

Name _____

3 →

4 ♥

5 ✋

6 ☕

7 🌲

8 🚩

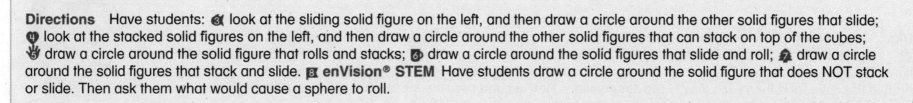

Directions Have students: **3** look at the sliding solid figure on the left, and then draw a circle around the other solid figures that slide; **4** look at the stacked solid figures on the left, and then draw a circle around the other solid figures that can stack on top of the cubes; **5** draw a circle around the solid figure that rolls and stacks; **6** draw a circle around the solid figures that slide and roll; **7** draw a circle around the solid figures that stack and slide. **8 enVision® STEM** Have students draw a circle around the solid figure that does NOT stack or slide. Then ask them what would cause a sphere to roll.

Independent Practice

Directions Have students: ✏ look at the rolling object on the left, and then draw a circle around the other objects that roll; 🏠 look at the sliding object on the left, and then draw a circle around the other objects that slide. ✿ **Higher Order Thinking** Have students draw 2 solid figures that can stack on each other. ✿ **Higher Order Thinking** Have students draw a circle around the cube, and then explain why the other solid is NOT a cube.

     Topic 13 | Lesson 2

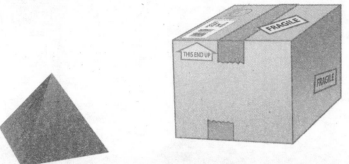

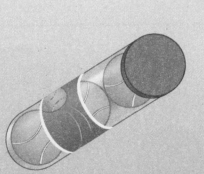

Directions Say: Jackson needs to find a circle that is a flat surface of a solid figure. Which of these solids has a flat circle as part of the figure? Draw a circle around each solid figure that has a flat circle part. Mark an X on the solid figures that do NOT have a flat circle part. How many shapes in all are there on the page? How many shapes did you circle? Without counting, how many shapes have an X? Count the shapes with an X to check your answer.

I can ...
analyze and compare 2-D and 3-D shapes.

© **Content Standards** K.G.B.4 Also K.OA.A.4
Mathematical Practices MP.2, MP.5, and MP.6

☆ Guided Practice

1

2

Directions Have students: **1** and **2** look at the shape on the left, and then draw a circle around the solid figures that have a flat surface with that shape.

Topic 13 | Lesson 3

3

4

5

6

Directions **3** **Vocabulary** Have students draw the **flat surface** of the solid figures that have circles around them. **4**–**6** Have students look at the shape on the left, and then draw a circle around the solid figures that have a flat surface with that shape.

Topic 13 | Lesson 3   five hundred nineteen **519**

Independent Practice

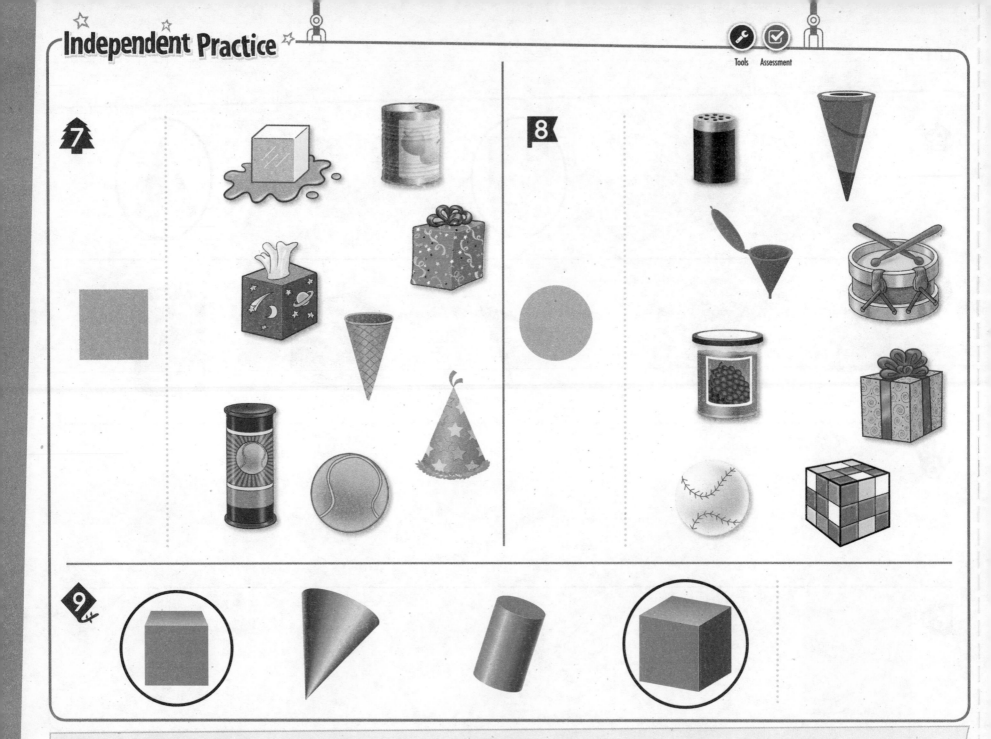

7

8

9

Directions Have students: **7** and **8** look at the shape on the left, and then draw a circle around the objects that have a flat surface with that shape. **9 Higher Order Thinking** Have students look at the solid figures that have a circle around them, and then draw the shape of the flat surfaces of these solid figures.

Topic 13 | Lesson 3

Name _____

Activity

1 flat

2 solid

Think.

Directions Say: *Jackson wants to put flat shapes behind Door 1 and solid figures behind Door 2. Draw a line from each shape to the correct door to show how he should sort the shapes. Count all the shapes on the shelves. Then cover one door. Count the number of shapes that are behind the door you can see. Without counting tell how many shapes you think are behind the other door. Then count to check your answer.*

I can ...
make sense of problems about shapes.

© **Mathematical Practices** MP.1
Also MP.3, MP.6
Content Standards K.G.B.4
Also K.OA.A.4, K.G.A.3

Visual Learning
 A-Z Glossary

Visual Learning Bridge

☆ Guided Practice

1

2

Directions Have students listen to the clues, mark an X on the shapes that do NOT fit the clues, and then draw a circle around the shape that the clues describe. Have students name the shape, and then explain their answers. **1** *I am a solid figure. I can roll. I have only 1 flat surface. What shape am I? Explain which clues helped you solve the mystery.* **2** *I am a solid figure. I can roll. I can also stack. What shape am I? Explain which clues helped you solve the mystery.*

522 five hundred twenty-two

Topic 13 | Lesson 4

Name _____

Tools Assessment

Independent Practice

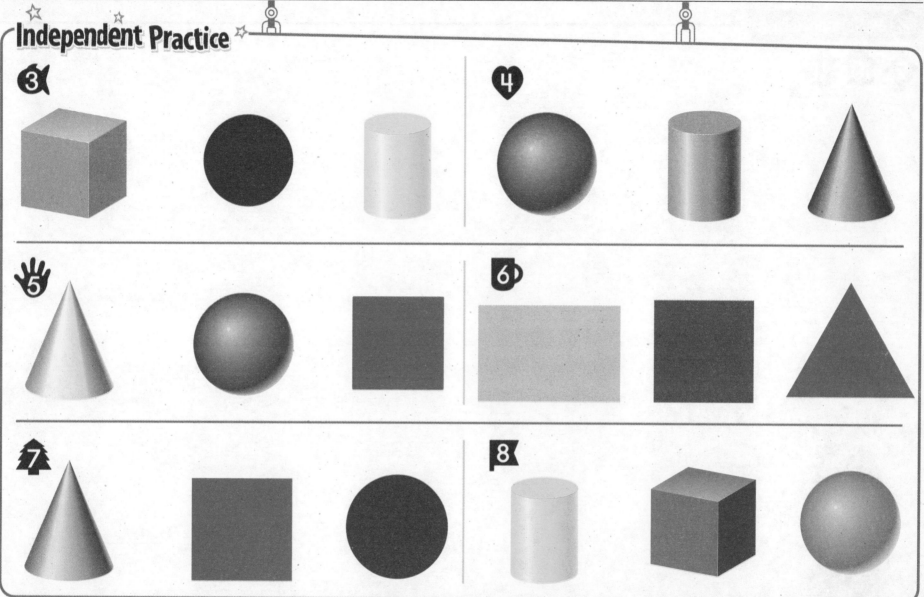

3 ★

4 ♥

5 ✋

6 ☕

7 🌲

8 🚩

Directions Have students listen to the clues, mark an X on the shapes that do NOT fit the clues, and then draw a circle around the shape that the clues describe. Have students name the shape, and then explain their answers. **3** *I am a solid figure. I can stack and slide. I have 6 flat surfaces. What shape am I?* **4** *I am a solid figure. I can slide. I have only 1 flat surface. What shape am I?* **5** *I am a solid figure. I can roll. I do NOT have any flat surfaces. What shape am I?* **6** *I am a flat shape. I have 4 sides. All of my sides are the same length. What shape am I?* **7** *I am a flat shape. I do NOT have any straight sides. What shape am I?* **8** *I am a solid figure. I can roll. I have 2 flat surfaces. What shape am I?*

Problem Solving

Directions Read the problem to students. Then have them use multiple problem-solving methods to solve the problem. Have students look at the shape at the top of the page. Say: *Emily's teacher teaches the class a game. They have to give a classmate clues about the mystery shape. What clues can Emily give about this shape?* **Make Sense** *What is the shape? What makes it special?* **Be Precise** *What clues can you give about the shape? Think about how it looks, and whether or not it can roll, stack, or slide.* **Explain** *What if your classmate gives you the wrong answer? Can you give more clues to help him or her?*

524 five hundred twenty-four

Solve & Share

Name _____

Directions Say: *Emily has 4 triangles. She thinks she can use them to make other 2-D shapes by matching the sides exactly AND by connecting the 4 triangle shapes by their sides only. Use 4 yellow triangles like the ones Emily is holding. Make as many different shapes as you can using all 4 triangles. As you make each shape, tell what shape you made or describe it and tell where the triangles are. Then draw all four triangles on your page to show your favorite shape.*

I can ...
make 2-D shapes using other 2-D shapes.

© **Content Standards** K.G.B.6 Also K.CC.B.5, K.G.A.1, K.G.B.5 **Mathematical Practices** MP.4, MP.7, and MP.8

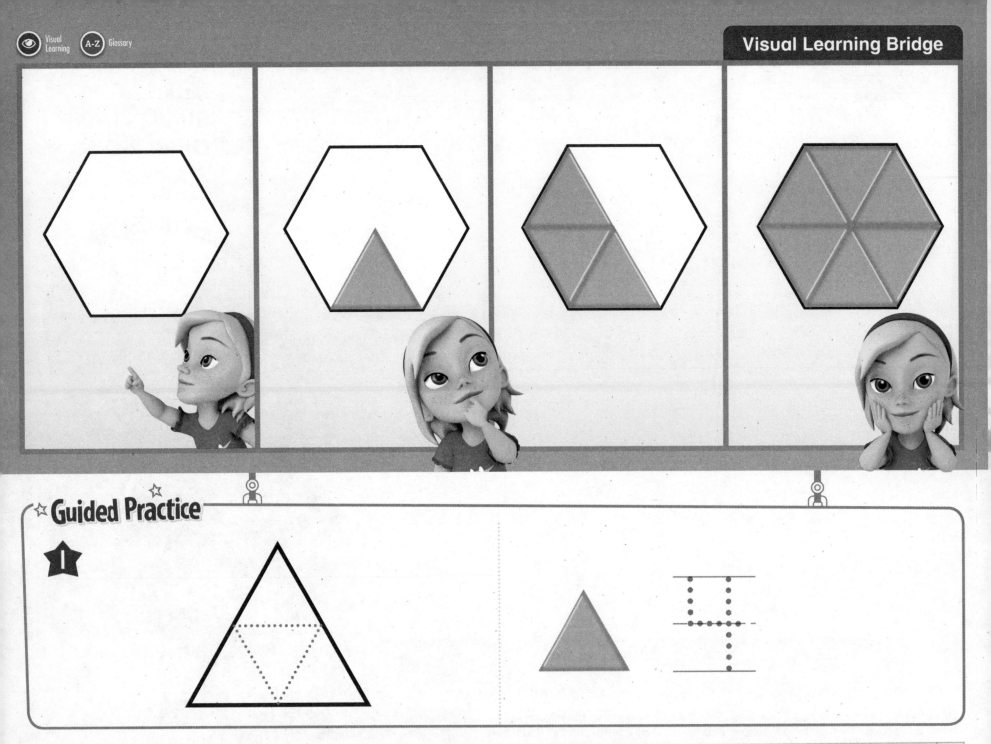

⭐ **Guided Practice**

⭐1

Directions ⭐ Have students use the pattern block shown to cover the shape, draw the lines, and then write the number that tells how many pattern blocks to use.

526 five hundred twenty-six

Topic 13 | Lesson 5

Name _____

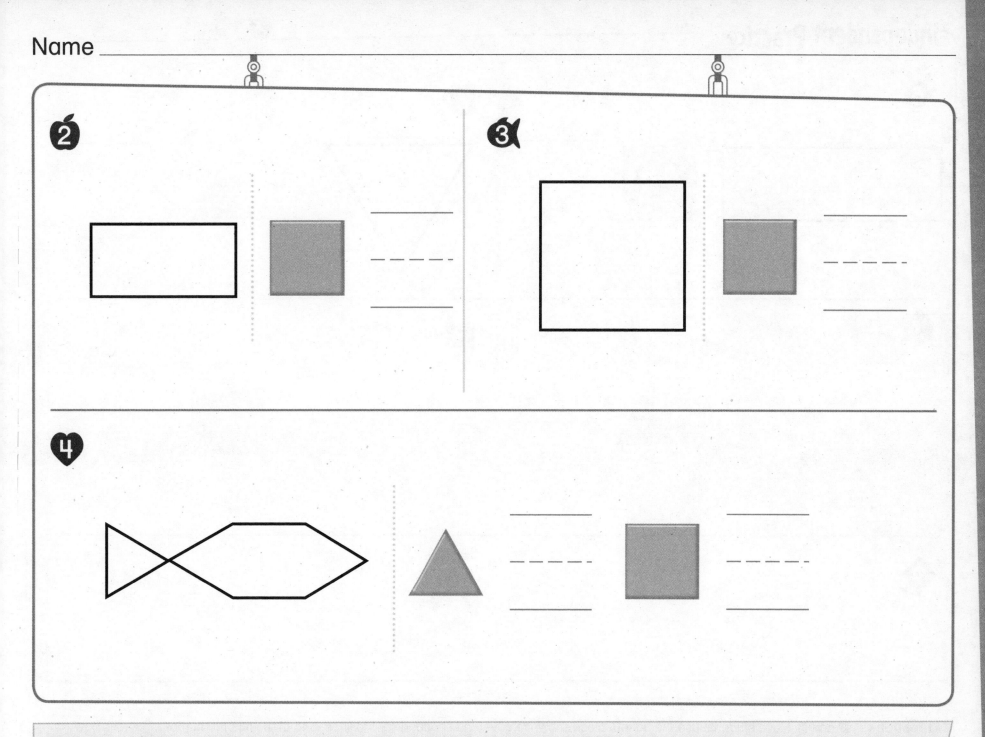

Topic 13 | Lesson 5

Directions ❷–❸ Have students use the pattern block shown to cover the shape, draw the lines, and then write the number that tells how many pattern blocks to use. ❹ Have students use the pattern blocks shown to create the fish, and then write the number that tells how many of each pattern block to use.

five hundred twenty-seven **527**

Independent Practice

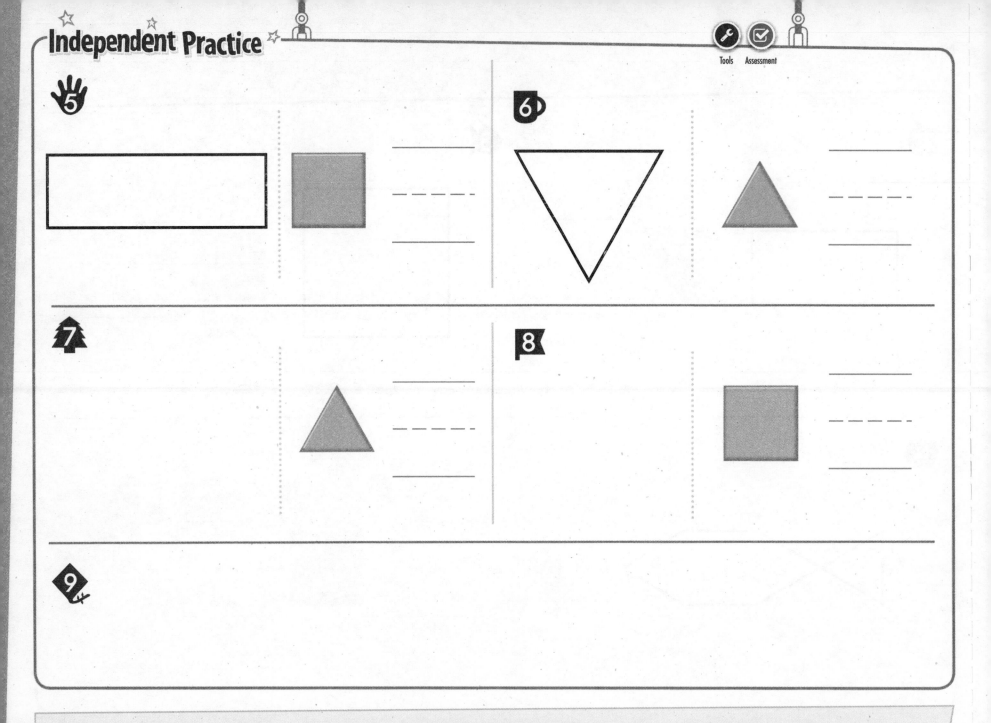

5

6

7

8

9

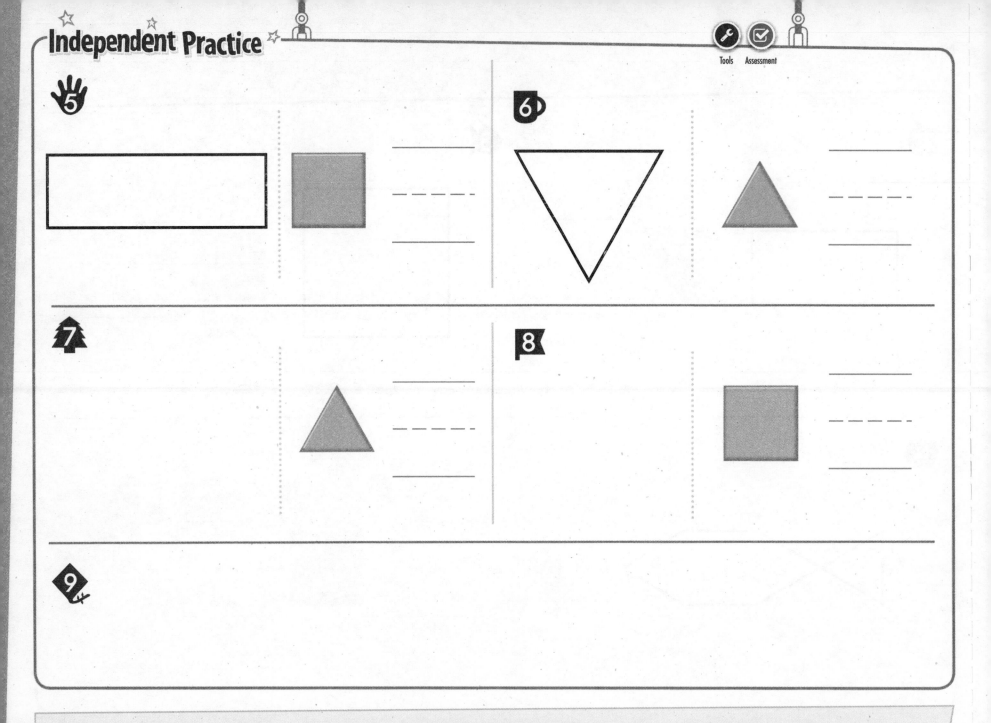

Directions ✋ and ☕ Have students use the pattern block shown to cover the shape, draw the lines, and then write the number that tells how many pattern blocks to use. 🌲 and 🚩 Have students use the pattern block shown to create a 2-D shape, draw the shape, and then write the number of pattern blocks used. 🔷 **Higher Order Thinking** Have students use pattern blocks to create a picture, and then draw it in the space.

528 five hundred twenty-eight

Copyright © SAVVAS Learning Company LLC. All Rights Reserved.

Topic 13 | Lesson 5

Name _____

 Activity

Circle

NOT a Circle

Directions Say: *Use yarn, string, or pipe cleaners to build a circle. Then use yarn, string, pipe cleaners, or straws to build a shape that is NOT a circle, and then tell what shape you built. Explain how the shapes you built are different from one another.*

I can ...
build 2-D shapes that match given attributes.

© **Content Standards** K.G.B.5 Also K.CC.B.5, K.G.B.4 **Mathematical Practices** MP.3, MP.5, and MP.7

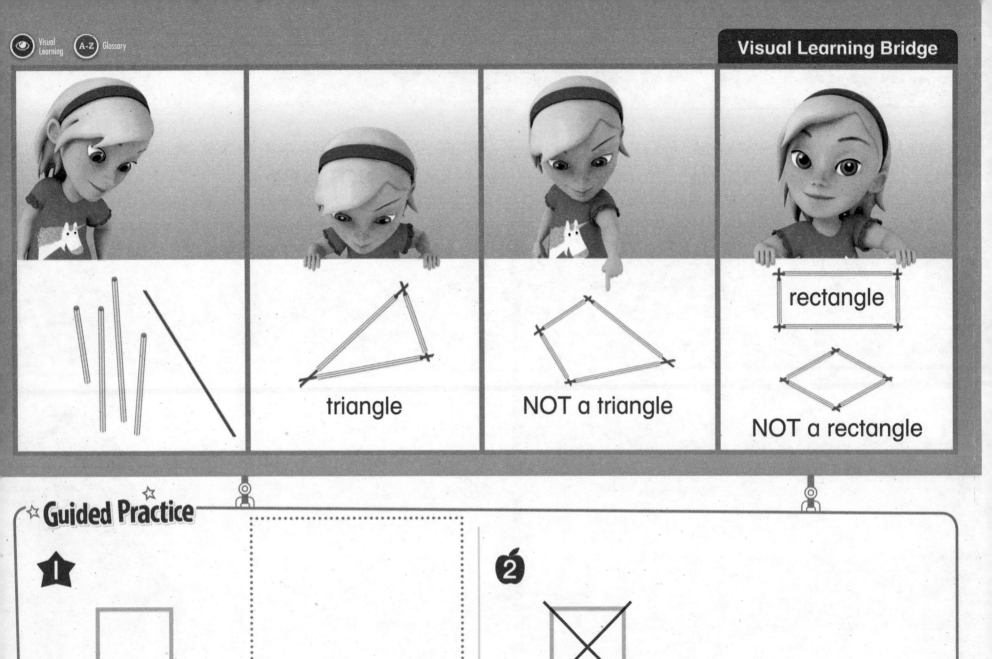

triangle

NOT a triangle

rectangle

NOT a rectangle

☆ **Guided Practice**

⭐ 1

🍎 2

Directions Provide students with yarn, pipe cleaners, or straws to make each shape. Students should attach the shapes they make with materials to the page. Have students draw or build: ⭐ a square; 🍎 a shape that is NOT a square.

Topic 13 | Lesson 6

Name _____

3

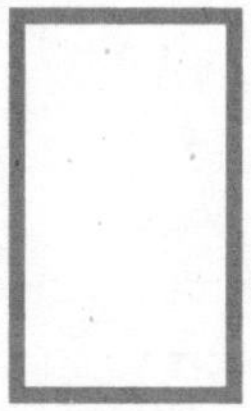

4

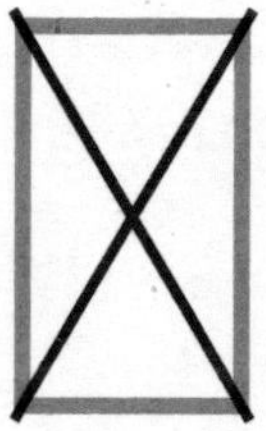

5

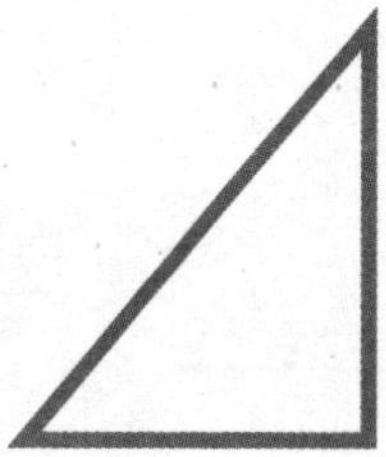

6

Directions Provide students with yarn, pipe cleaners, or straws to make each shape. Students should attach the shapes they make with materials to the page. Have students draw or build: **3** a rectangle; **4** a shape that is NOT a rectangle; **5** a triangle; **6** a shape that is NOT a triangle.

Topic 13 | Lesson 6   five hundred thirty-one **531**

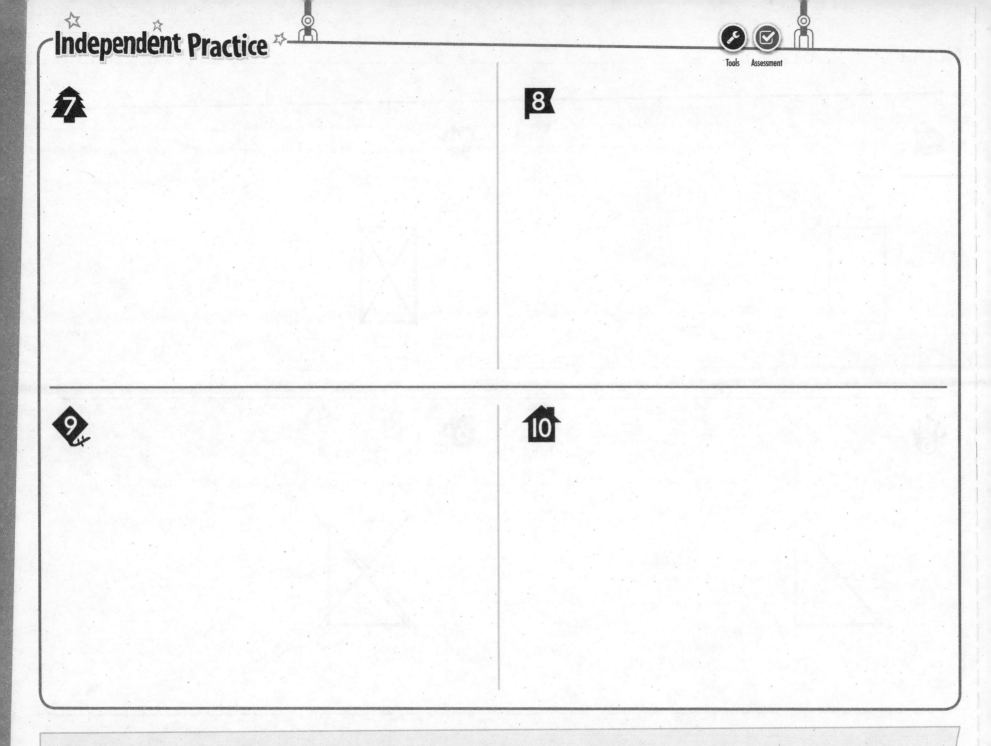

7

8

9

10

Solve & Share

Activity

Lesson 13-7
Build 3-D Shapes

I can ...
use materials to build 3-D shapes.

© **Content Standards** K.G.B.5, K.G.B.6 Also K.CC.B.5 **Mathematical Practices** MP.2, MP.5, and MP.6

Directions Say: *Jackson wants to build this building with solid figures. Which solid figures can he use? Tell how you know.*

☆ Guided Practice

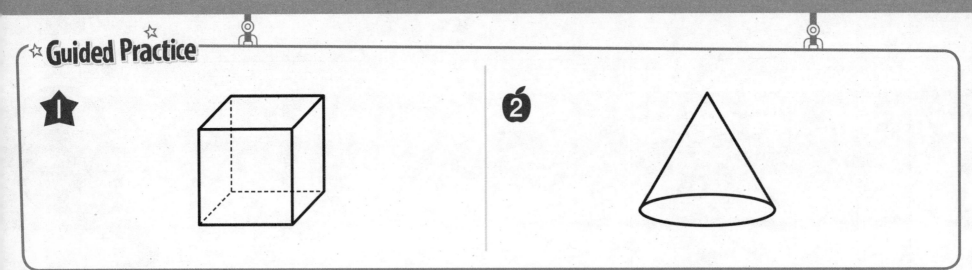

1

2

Directions 1 and 2 Have students use straws, clay, craft sticks, paper, or other materials to build the solid figure shown.

Topic 13 | Lesson 7

Name _____

3

4

5

6

Directions Have students: **3** and **4** use tools to build the shape, and then draw a circle around the solid figures that build the shape; **5** and **6** use tools to find the shape the solid figures can build, and then draw a circle around the shape.

Topic 13 | Lesson 7   five hundred thirty-five **535**

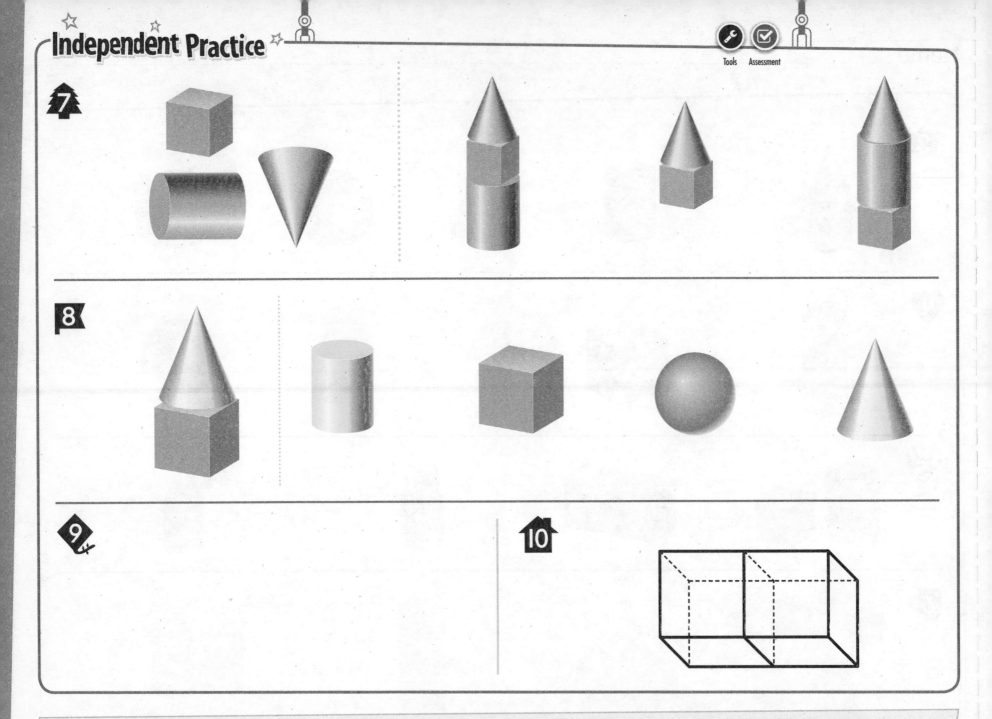

7

8

9

10

Directions Have students: **7** use tools to find the shape the solid figures can build, and then draw a circle around the shapes; **8** use tools to build the shape, and then draw a circle around the solid figures that build the shape. **9 Higher Order Thinking** Have students use straws, yarn, pipe cleaners, or other materials to build a solid figure that is NOT a cone. Say: *Draw a sketch of the solid figure you made.* **10 Higher Order Thinking** Have students use straws, clay, craft sticks, paper, or other materials to build the shape shown.

Find a Match Name _____

TOPIC 13

Fluency Practice Activity

1

P	T	O
1 + 0	5 − 2	3 + 2

___ ___ ___	___ ___ ___	___ ___ ___
1 + 2	4 + 1	4 − 3

2

T	H	A
5 − 1	1 + 1	2 − 2

___ ___ ___	___ ___ ___	___ ___ ___
3 − 1	5 − 5	2 + 2

Directions **1** and **2** Have students find a partner. Have them point to a clue in the top row, and then solve the addition or subtraction problem in the clue. Then have them look at the clues in the bottom row to find a match, and then write the clue letter above the match. Have students find a match for every clue.

I can ...
add and subtract fluently within 5.

© **Content Standard** K.OA.A.5
Mathematical Practices MP.3, MP.6, MP.7, and MP.8

1

2

3

Directions **Understand Vocabulary** Have students: ⭐ draw a circle around the solid figures that **roll**; 🍎 draw a circle around the solid figures that **stack**; 🐟 draw a circle around the solid figures that **slide**.

538 five hundred thirty-eight

Name _____

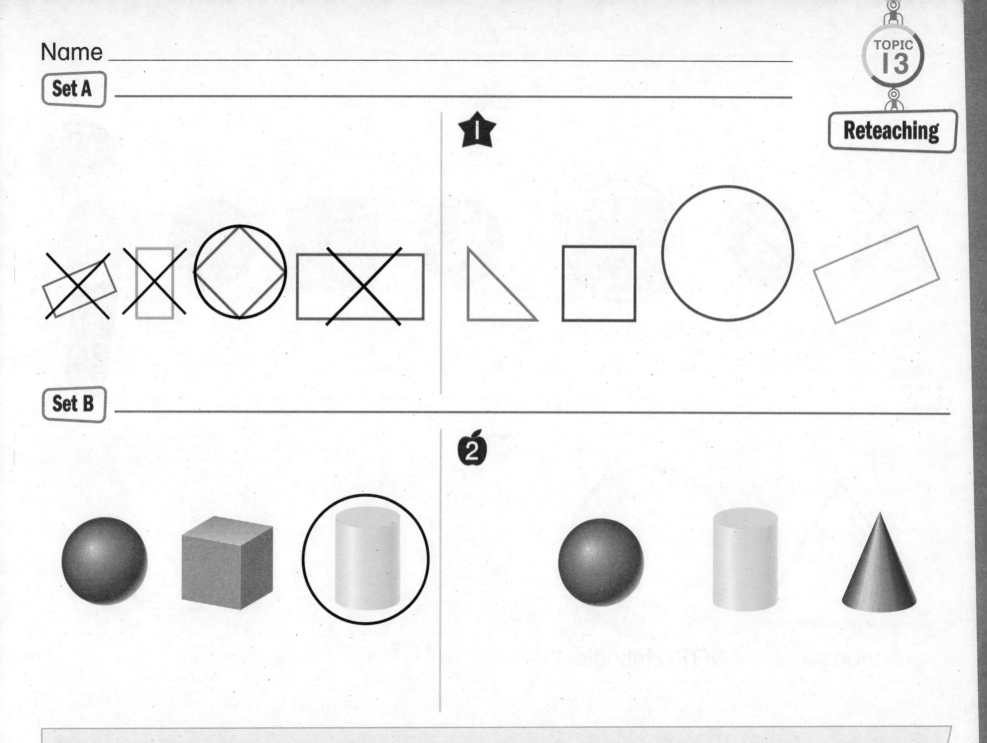

⭐ 1

Set B

🍎 2

Directions Have students: ⭐ listen to the clues, mark an X on the shapes that do NOT fit the clues, draw a circle around the shape that the clues describe, and then tell how the shapes they marked with an X are similar to the shape they drew a circle around. *I am NOT round. I have 4 sides. They are NOT all the same length;* 🍎 draw a circle around the solid figure that does NOT stack and slide.

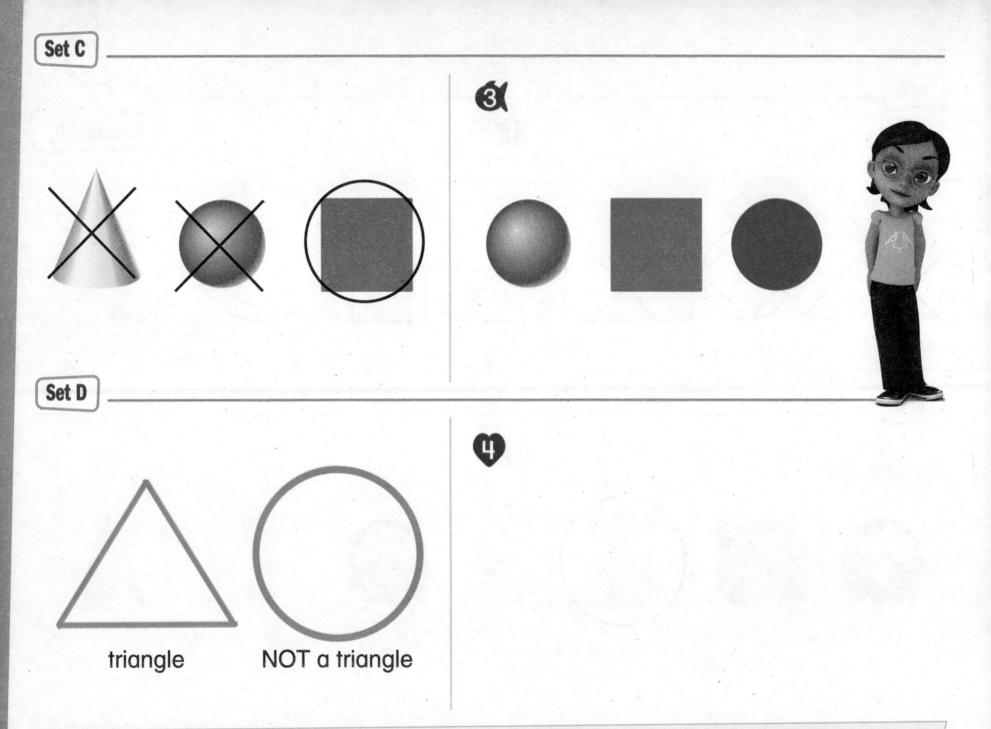

③

triangle   NOT a triangle

④

Directions Have students: ③ mark an X on the shapes that do NOT fit the clues, and then draw a circle around the shape the clues describe: *I have no sides. I do NOT roll. Which shape am I?* ④ draw or use yarn, pipe cleaners, or straws to make a triangle and a shape that is NOT a triangle, and then attach their shapes to this page.

Name _____

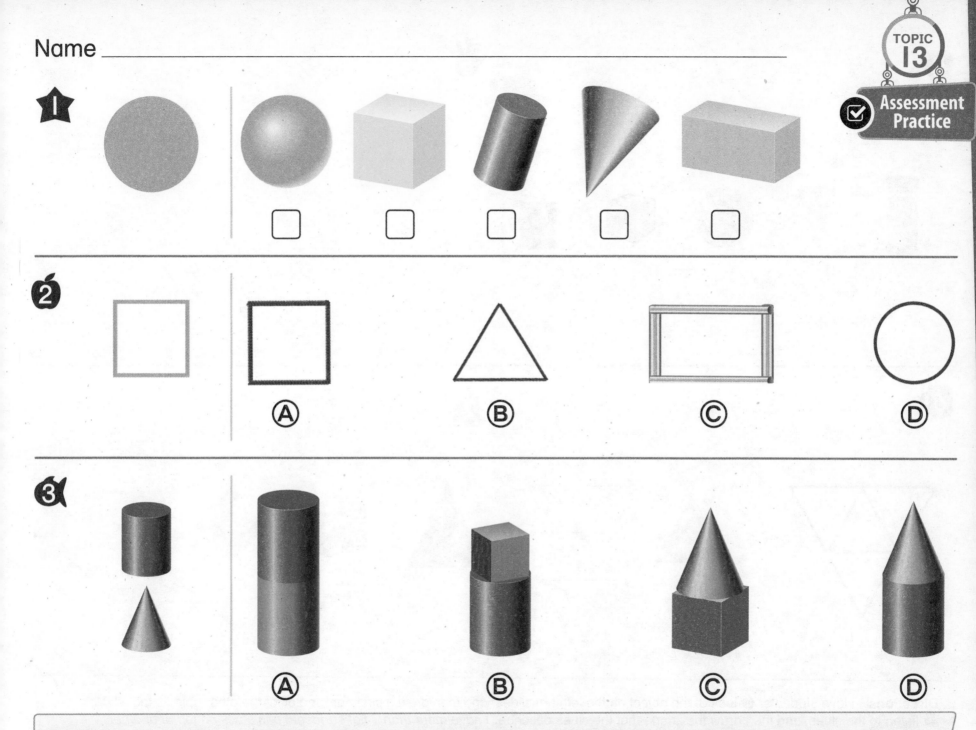

⭐ 1

🍎 2

Ⓐ   Ⓑ   Ⓒ   Ⓓ

🐟 3

Ⓐ   Ⓑ   Ⓒ   Ⓓ

Directions Have students mark the best answer. ⭐ Look at the shape on the left. Mark the two solid figures that have a flat surface with that same shape. 🍎 Which shape that was built using different materials or drawn matches the shape on the left? 🐟 Which shape can be built using the solid figures on the left?

 →

 6

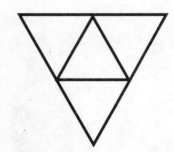

7

Directions Have students: **4** look at the object on the left that slides, and then draw a circle around all of the other objects that slide; **5** listen to the clues, and then draw the shape that the clues describe. *I have more than 1 flat surface. I can stack on top of another shape. I can roll. What solid figure am I?*; **6** write the number that tells how many triangle pattern blocks can cover the shape; **7** listen to the clues, mark an X on the shapes that do NOT fit the clues, and then draw a circle around the shape that the clues describe. *I am a flat shape. I have 4 straight sides. Two of my sides are shorter than the other 2 sides. What shape am I?*

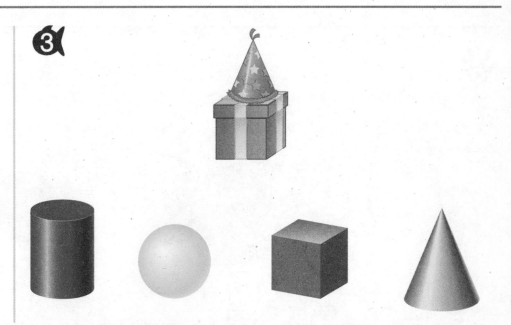

Directions **Bria's Bash** Say: *Bria has a party for her friends. These are some objects that are at her party.* Have students: ★ draw a circle around the objects that can slide. Have them tell how the shapes of those objects are different from the shapes of the other objects. Then have students mark an X on the objects that are cylinders. ② draw what one flat surface of a cylinder looks like, and then name that shape. ③ Say: *Bria puts her party hat on top of a present.* Have students draw a circle around the solid figures that could be used to build the same shape. If needed, have students use tools to help them.

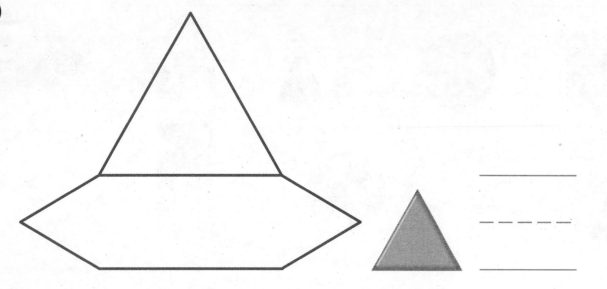

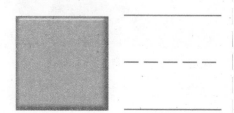

Directions 4 Say: *Bria makes a puzzle for her friends. She uses pattern blocks to make this spaceship. Show how Bria makes her puzzle.* Have students use pattern blocks to cover, and then draw lines on the spaceship. Have them write the number that tells how many of each pattern block they used. 5 Say: *Bria plays a game at her party. She gives her friends clues and has them tell her what object she is thinking about. Bria gives these clues:* The object is NOT a solid shape. The object is NOT round. The object has 3 sides. Have students mark an X on each object that does NOT fit the clues, draw a circle around the object that Bria describes, and then name the shape of that object.

Copyright © SAVVAS Learning Company LLC. All Rights Reserved.

Topic 13 | Performance Task

Describe and Compare Measurable Attributes

Essential Question: How can objects be described and compared by length, height, capacity, and weight?

Shade

Structures provide shade.

enVision STEM Project: Using Materials to Create Shade

Directions Read the character speech bubbles to students. **Find Out!** Have students find out different ways to create shade. Say: *We can use materials to create shade. Talk to your friends and relatives about different ways humans create shade from the sun.* **Journal: Make a Poster** Have students make a poster that shows various objects humans use to create shade. Have them draw three different ways humans create shade.

Name _____

Review What You Know

1 ⭐

2 🍎

3 🐦

4 💜

5 ✋

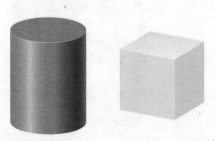

6 ☕

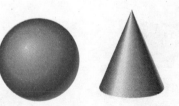

Directions Have students: ⭐ draw a circle around the cube; 🍎 draw a circle around the cylinder; 🐦 draw a circle around the cone; 💜 draw a circle around the solid figure that can stack; ✋ draw a circle around the solid figure that can roll; ☕ draw a circle around the solid figure that can slide.

Name _____

A

B

Directions Say: *You will choose one of these projects. Look at picture **A**. Think about this question: Do you know how much you have grown since you were a baby? If you choose Project A, you will make a display about hand size. Look at picture **B**. Think about this question: What type of art is this? If you choose Project B, you will build a straw sculpture.*

Directions Say: *You will choose one of these projects. Look at picture* **C.** *Think about this question: Would you want to be the tallest person in the world? If you choose Project C, you will trace footprints and measure. Look at picture* **D.** *Think about this question: What is the largest animal on Earth? If you choose Project D, you will create a mammals poster.*

Name _____

Activity

Describe and Compare by Length and Height

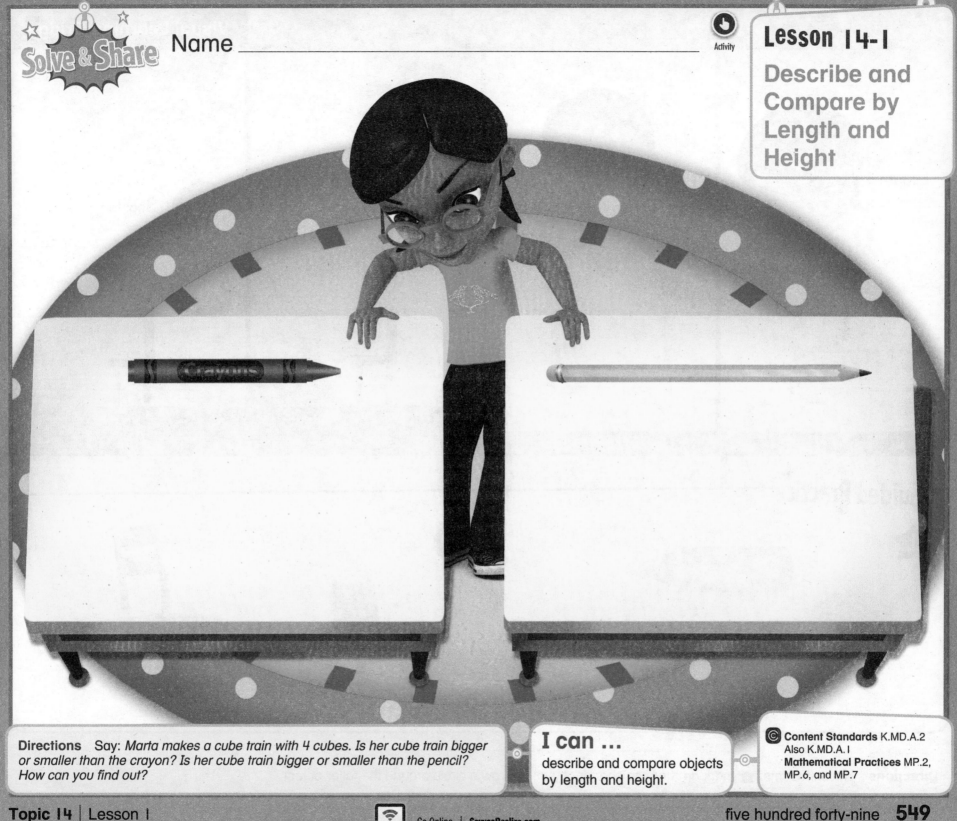

Directions Say: *Marta makes a cube train with 4 cubes. Is her cube train bigger or smaller than the crayon? Is her cube train bigger or smaller than the pencil? How can you find out?*

I can ...
describe and compare objects by length and height.

© **Content Standards** K.MD.A.2 Also K.MD.A.1
Mathematical Practices MP.2, MP.6, and MP.7

Go Online | SavvasRealize.com

☆ Guided Practice

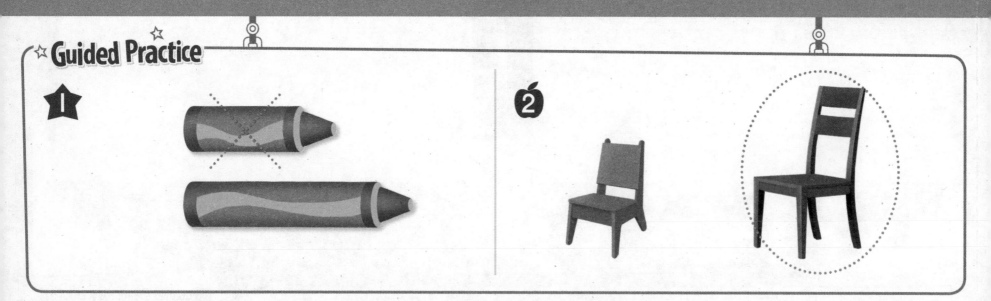

Directions Have students: ① mark an X on the shorter object; ② draw a circle around the taller object.

Name _____

3

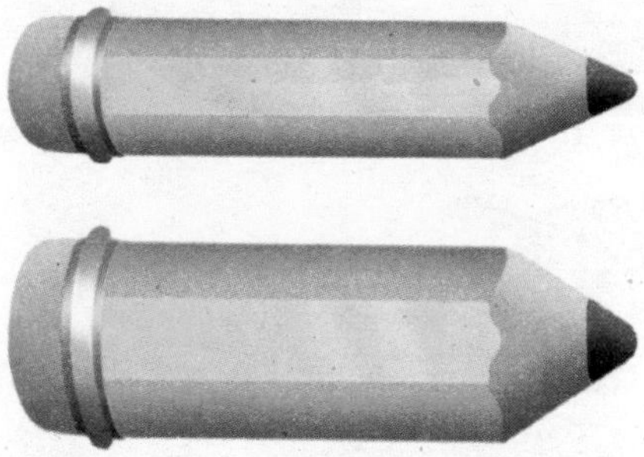

4

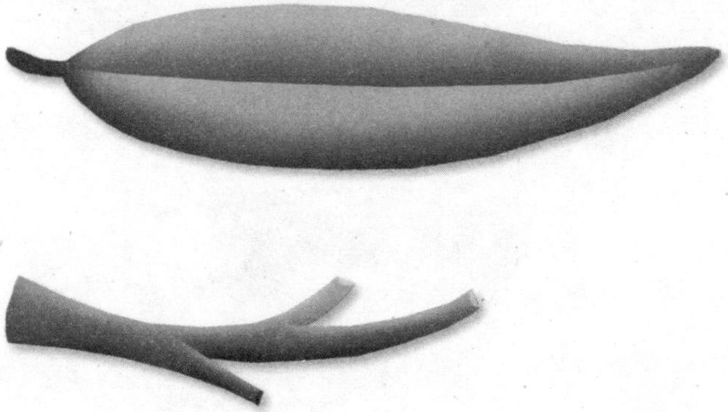

5

6

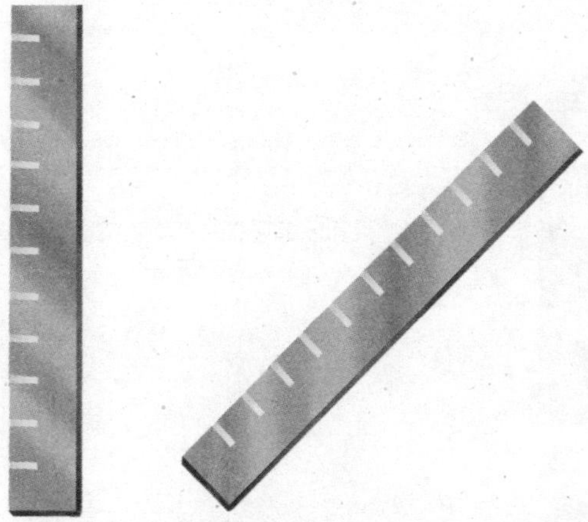

Directions Have students: **3** and **4** draw a circle around the longer object or underline the objects if they are the same length; **5** and **6** mark an X on the shorter object or underline the objects if they are the same height.

Independent Practice

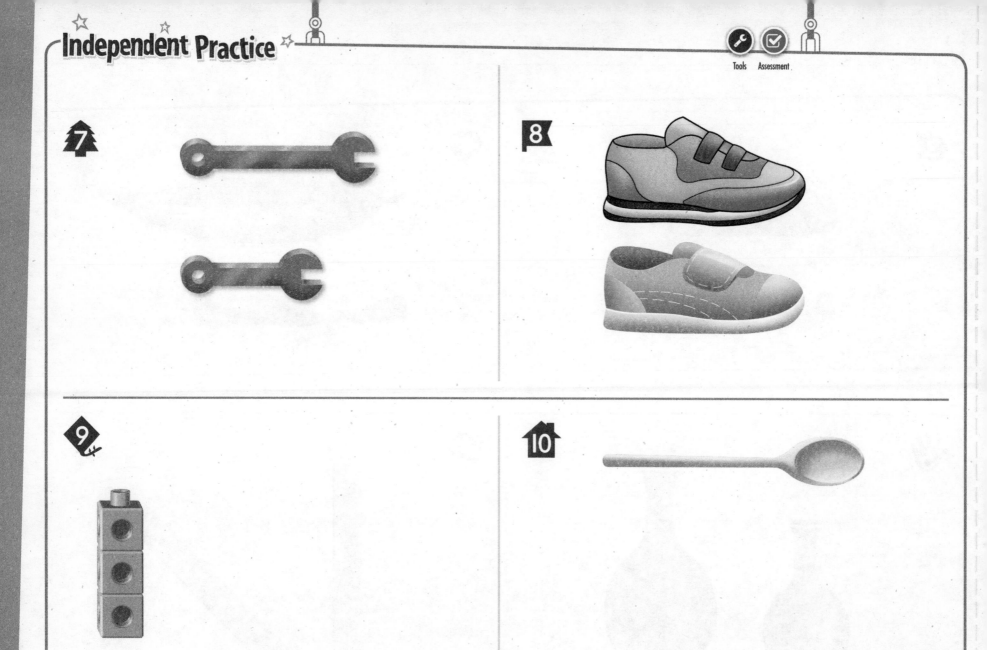

7

8

9

10

Directions 7 and 8 Have students mark an X on the shorter object and draw a circle around the longer object, or underline the objects if they are the same length. 9 **Higher Order Thinking** Have students draw an object that is shorter than the cube tower. 10 **Higher Order Thinking** Have students draw an object that is the same length as the spoon.

Topic 14 | Lesson 1

Name _____

Directions Say: *Marta has 2 cups. She wants to use the cup that holds more. How can she find out which cup holds more? Glue the cup that holds less on the left side of the workmat and the cup that holds more on the right side.*

I can ...
describe and compare objects by capacity.

© **Content Standards** K.MD.A.2 Also K.MD.A.1
Mathematical Practices MP.2, MP.3, and MP.8

Holds more

Holds less

Holds the same

☆ Guided Practice

1

2

Directions ★ and ② Have students draw a circle around the cup that holds more and mark an X on the cup that holds less, or underline the cups if they hold the same amount.

Topic 14 | Lesson 2

Name _____

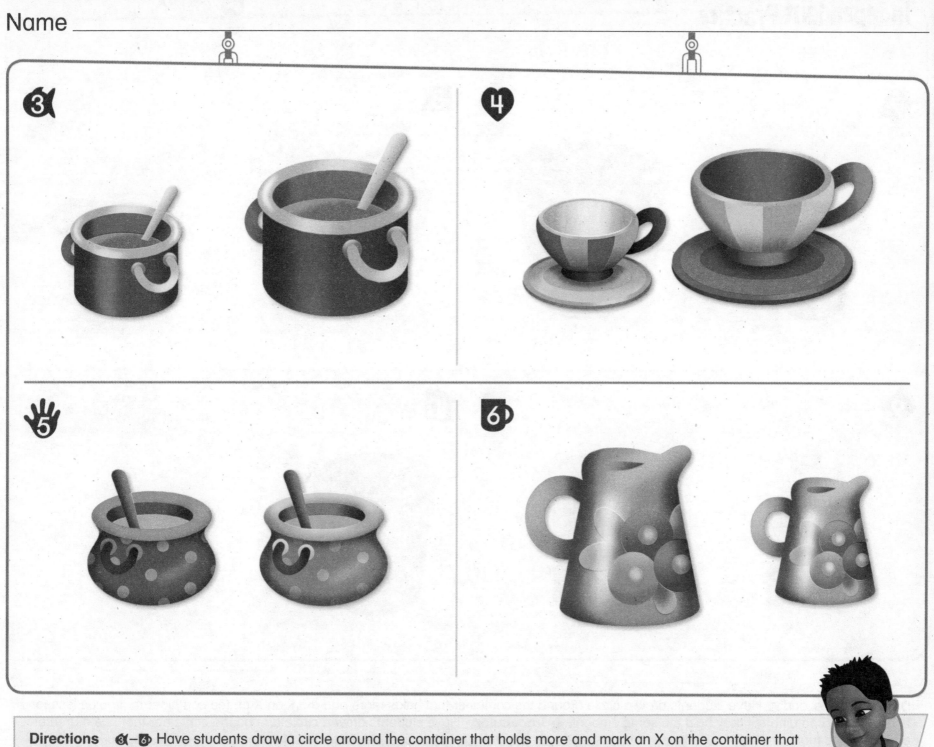

3

4

5

6

Directions ❸–❻ Have students draw a circle around the container that holds more and mark an X on the container that holds less, or underline the containers if they hold the same amount.

Topic 14 | Lesson 2

five hundred fifty-five **555**

Independent Practice

7

8

9

10

Directions 7 and 8 Have students draw a circle around the container that holds more and mark an X on the container that holds less, or underline the containers if they hold the same amount. **9 Vocabulary** Have students draw a circle around the container that has a greater **capacity** and mark an X on the container that has a smaller **capacity**, or underline the containers if they have the same **capacity**, and then explain how they know. **10 Higher Order Thinking** Have students draw a container that holds less than the container shown.

Topic 14 | Lesson 2

Directions Say: *Marta has a pencil and a book. She wants to put the lighter object in her backpack. How can she figure out which object is lighter? Draw the objects where they belong on the balance scale.*

I can ...
describe and compare objects by weight.

© **Content Standards** K.MD.A.2
Also K.MD.A.1
Mathematical Practices MP.2, MP.3, and MP.4

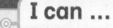
Go Online | SavvasRealize.com

Visual Learning · A-Z Glossary

Visual Learning Bridge

☆ Guided Practice

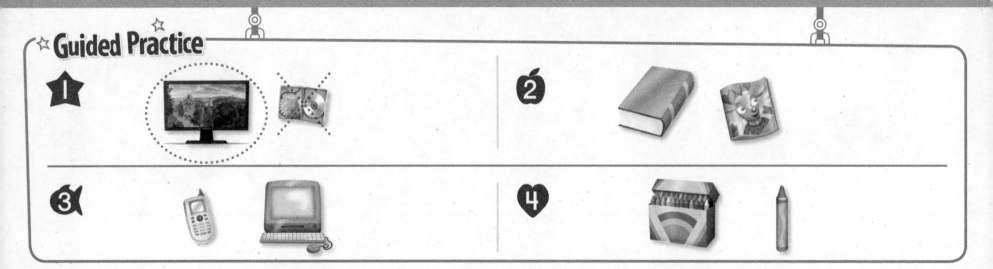

1

2

3

4

Directions **1**–**4** Have students draw a circle around the heavier object and mark an X on the lighter object, or underline the objects if they are the same weight.

558 five hundred fifty-eight

Topic 14 | Lesson 3

Name _____

5

6

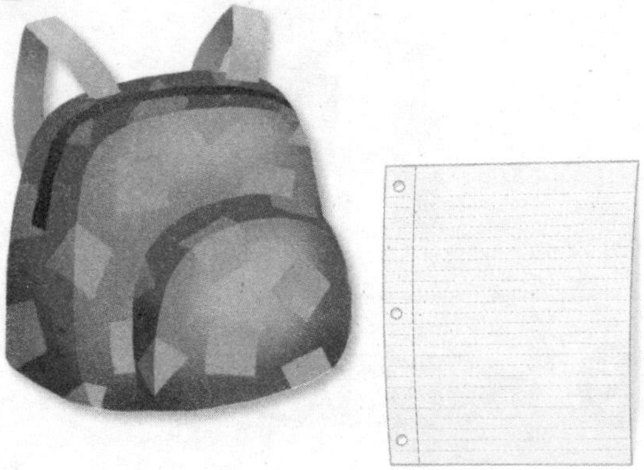

7

8

9

10

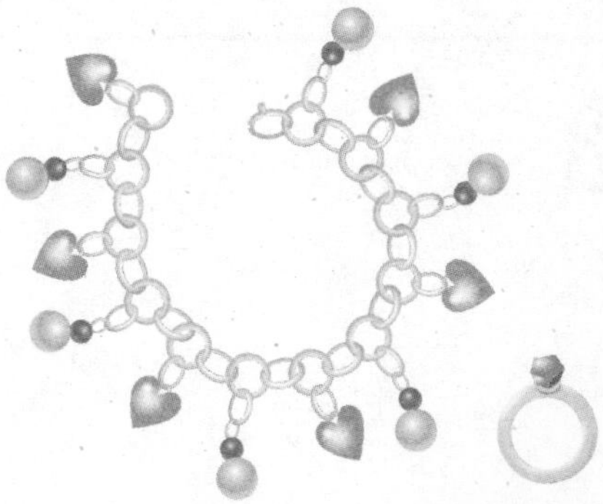

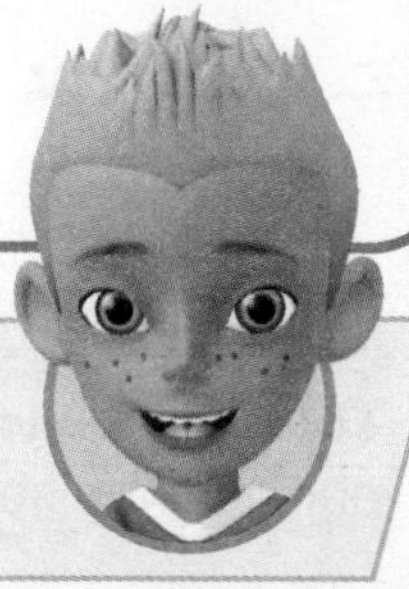

Directions 5–10 Have students draw a circle around the heavier object and mark an X on the lighter object, or underline the objects if they are the same weight.

Independent Practice

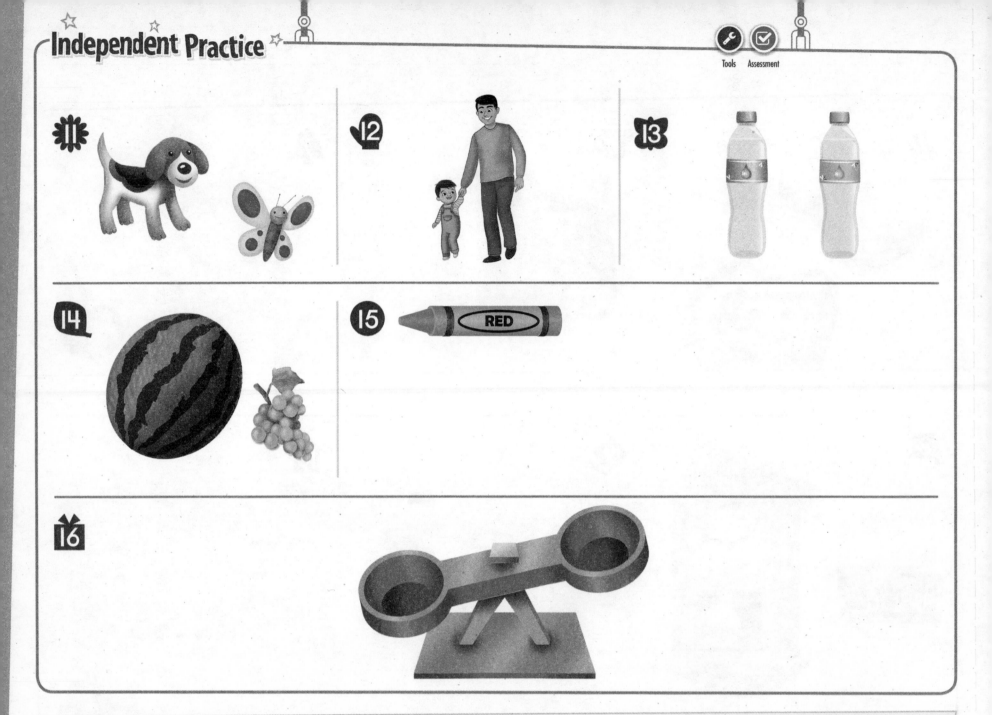

11

12

13

14

15 RED

16

Directions **11**–**14** Have students draw a circle around the heavier object and mark an X on the lighter object, or underline the objects if they are the same weight. **15 Vocabulary** Have students draw an object that is the same **weight** as the crayon. **16 Higher Order Thinking** Have students draw 2 objects. Have them draw the heavier object in the space next to the lower side of the scale and the lighter object in the space next to the higher side of the scale.

     Topic 14 | Lesson 3

Solve & Share

Activity

Describe Objects by Measurable Attributes

Directions Say: *These are 2 tools for measuring. What can you measure with the cup? What can you measure with the cube train? Draw an object you can measure with each tool.*

I can ...
use measurable attributes to describe different objects.

© **Content Standard** K.MD.A.1
Mathematical Practices MP.1, MP.2, and MP.5

Visual Learning   A-Z Glossary

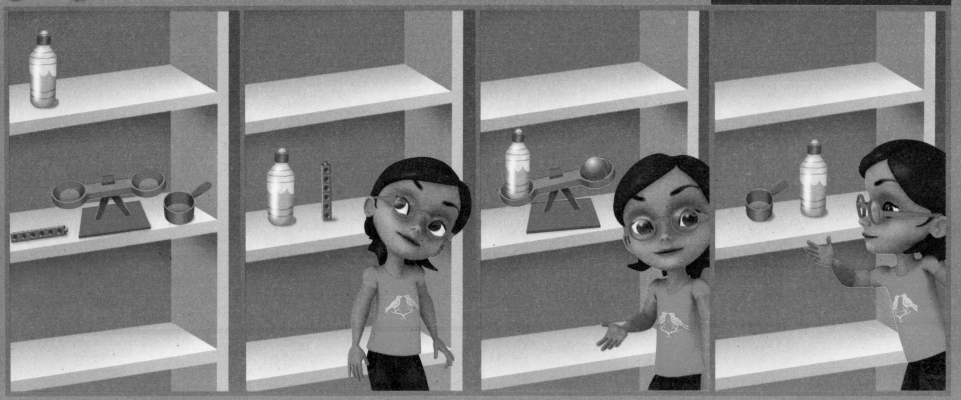

☆ Guided Practice

1

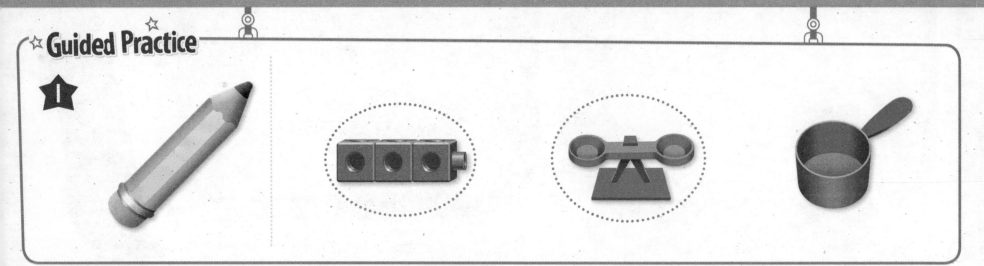

Directions ⭐ Have students look at the object on the left, identify the attributes that can be measured, and then draw a circle around the tools that could be used to tell about those attributes.

Name _____

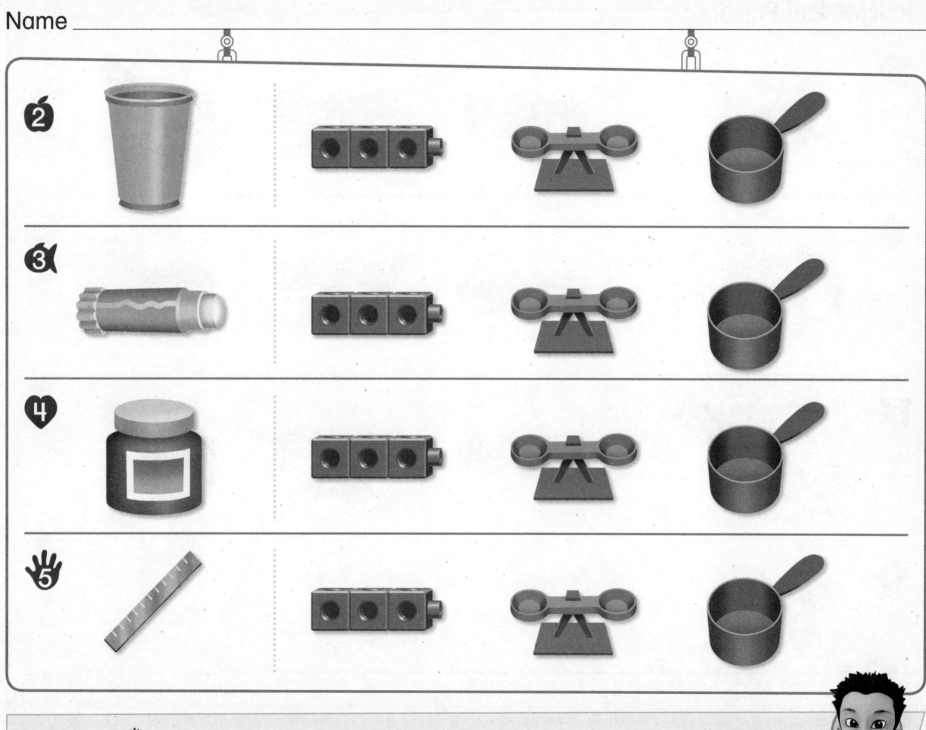

Directions 🍎–✋ Have students look at the object on the left, identify the attributes that can be measured, and then draw a circle around the tools that could be used to tell about those attributes.

Independent Practice

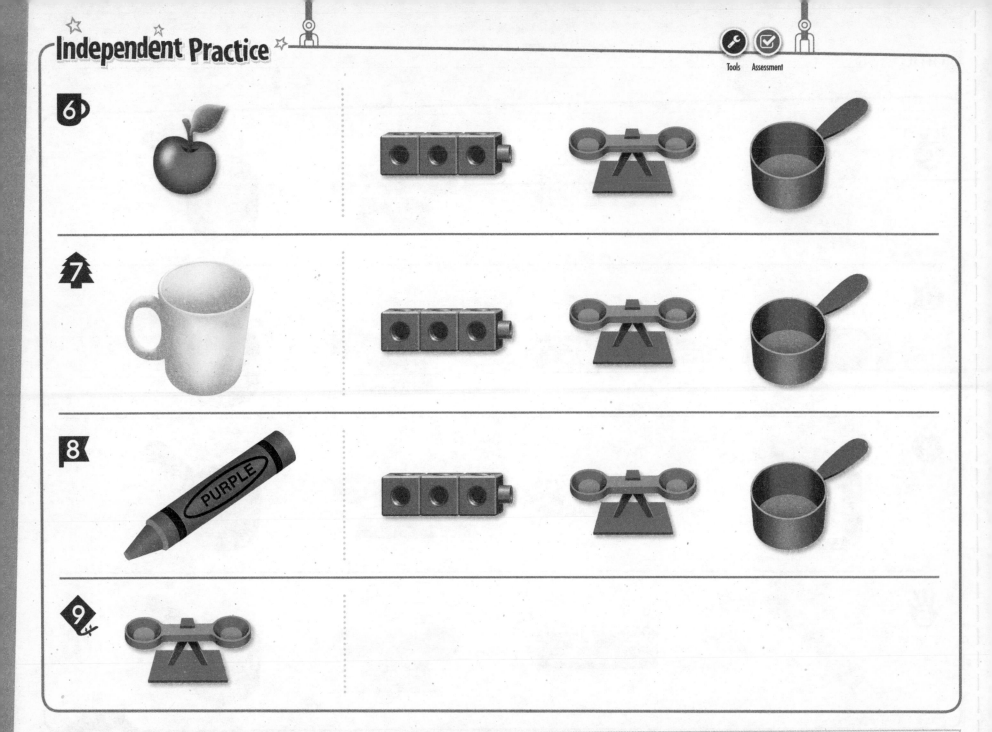

6

7

8

9

Directions **6–8** Have students look at the object on the left, identify the attributes that can be measured, and then draw a circle around the tools that could be used to tell about those attributes. **9 Higher Order Thinking** Have students identify the attribute that can be measured using the tool on the left, and then draw 2 objects that could be measured using that tool.

       Topic 14 | Lesson 4

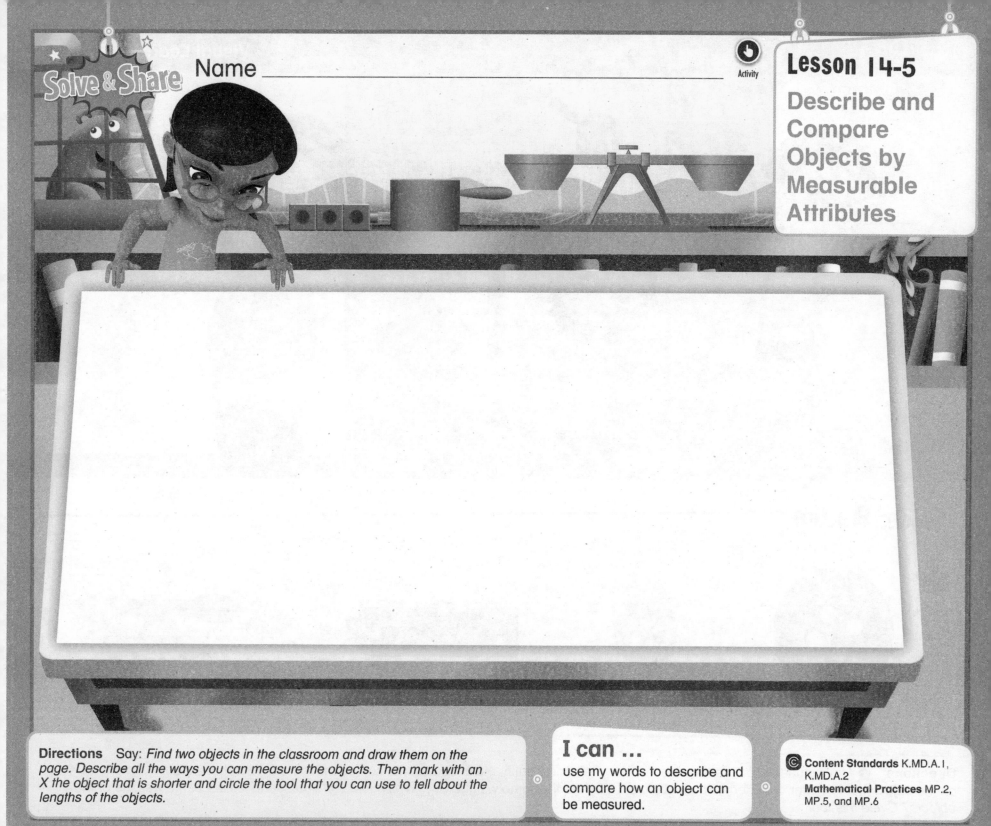

Activity

Lesson 14-5

Describe and Compare Objects by Measurable Attributes

Directions Say: *Find two objects in the classroom and draw them on the page. Describe all the ways you can measure the objects. Then mark with an X the object that is shorter and circle the tool that you can use to tell about the lengths of the objects.*

I can ...

use my words to describe and compare how an object can be measured.

© **Content Standards** K.MD.A.1, K.MD.A.2
Mathematical Practices MP.2, MP.5, and MP.6

Guided Practice

   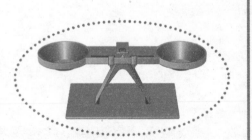

Directions ⭐ Have students look at the objects on the left and identify the attributes that can be measured. Then have students mark an X on the object that is lighter or underline both objects if they are the same weight. Say: *Which tool can you use to tell about the weights of the objects? Circle this tool.*

Topic 14 | Lesson 5

2

3

4

Directions Have students look at the objects on the left and identify the attributes that can be measured. **2**–**3** Then have students mark an X on the object that holds less or underline both objects if they can hold the same amount. Say: *Which tool can you use to tell about how much the objects hold? Circle this tool.* **4** Then have students circle the object that holds more or underline both objects if they can hold the same amount. Say: *Circle the tool that can be used to tell about how much an object holds. Explain how you know.*

Independent Practice

Directions 👋 and 🐚 Have students look at the objects on the left and identify the attributes that can be measured. Then have students draw a circle around the object that is heavier or underline both objects if they are the same weight. Say: *Which tool can you use to tell about the weights of the objects? Circle this tool.* 🌲 **Higher Order Thinking** On the left, have students draw an object that can be measured using the tool shown. On the right, have them draw an object that CANNOT be measured using the tool shown.

Solve & Share

Activity

Think.

3

Directions Say: *Marta wants to compare the length of a ribbon to the length of a cube train so she can draw a circle around the object that is shorter. How can she do this? Explain where you place the cube train on the page and why.*

I can ...
solve math problems about objects with measurable attributes by using precision.

© **Mathematical Practices** MP.6
Also MP.3, MP.5
Content Standard K.MD.A.2

Think.

Cubes

Compare.

7

Longer

☆ Guided Practice

1

5

2

1

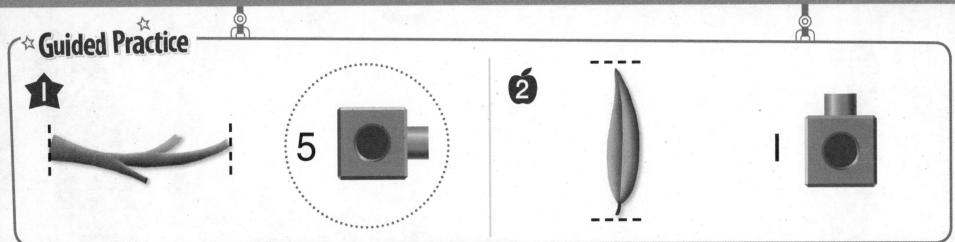

Directions Have students: ★ make a cube train with the number of cubes shown, compare the length of the cube train to the object, and then draw a circle around the one that is longer; ❷ make a cube tower with the number of cubes shown, compare the height of the cube tower to the object, and then draw a circle around the one that is taller.

Name _____

Independent Practice

3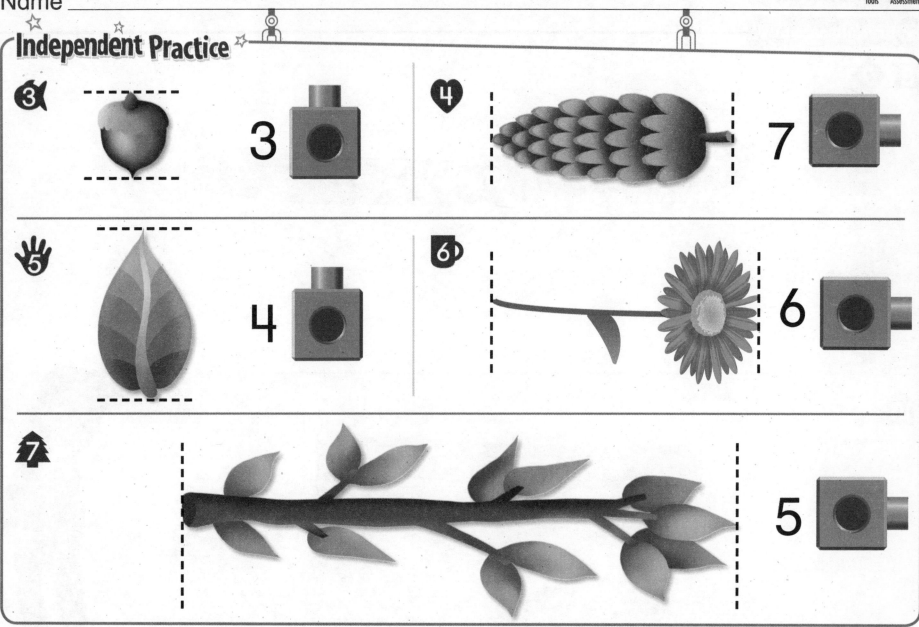

3

4

7

5

4

6

6

7

5

Directions Have students make a cube train or cube tower with the number of cubes shown. Then have them: **3** compare the height of the cube tower to the acorn, and then draw a circle around the one that is taller; **4** compare the length of the pinecone to the cube train and mark an X on the one that is shorter; **5** compare the height of the cube tower to the leaf, and then draw a circle around the one that is taller; **6** compare the length of the flower to the cube train and mark an X on the one that is shorter; **7** compare the length of the cube train to the twig, and then draw a circle around the one that is longer.

Problem Solving

_____

_ _ _ _ _ _

_____

Directions Read the problem aloud. Then have students use multiple problem-solving methods to solve the problem. Say: *Alex has a piece of ribbon. He wants to make a cube train longer than the ribbon. How many cubes long will the cube train be?* 🐝 **Use Tools** *What tool can you use to help solve the problem? Make a cube train that is longer than the piece of purple ribbon, and then write the number of cubes in the train. Explain your answer.* 🔷 **Be Precise** *Why is it important to count the cubes?* 🏠 **Explain** *Carlos says that he made a cube train that is 3 cubes long and that it is longer than the length of the orange ribbon. Is he right or wrong? How do you know?*

Topic 14 | Lesson 6

⭐ 1

5 − 1	2 + 3	1 + 2	1 + 1	4 − 4
5 − 5	1 + 4	0 + 1	0 + 3	2 + 1
2 − 1	5 + 0	5 − 3	1 + 3	3 − 0
4 + 0	3 + 2	5 − 2	5 − 4	2 + 0
1 − 1	0 + 5	2 + 3	4 + 1	5 − 0

 2

_____

_ _ _ _ _

_____

I can ...
add and subtract fluently within 5.

© **Content Standard** K.OA.A.5
Mathematical Practices MP.3,
MP.6, MP.7, and MP.8

Directions Have students: ⭐ color each box that has a sum or difference that is equal to 5; 2 write the letter that they see.

TOPIC 14 | Vocabulary Review
 Glossary

1

2

3

4

5

Directions **Understand Vocabulary** Have students: ★ draw a circle around the tool that measures **length**; ② draw a circle around the **longer** object; ③ mark an X on the pitcher that has a smaller **capacity**; ④ draw an object that is the same **height** as the cubes; ✋ draw a circle around the pair of animals that can be the same **weight**.

574 five hundred seventy-four

Copyright © SAVVAS Learning Company LLC. All Rights Reserved.

Topic 14 | Vocabulary Review

Name ______________________

TOPIC 14

Reteaching

Set A

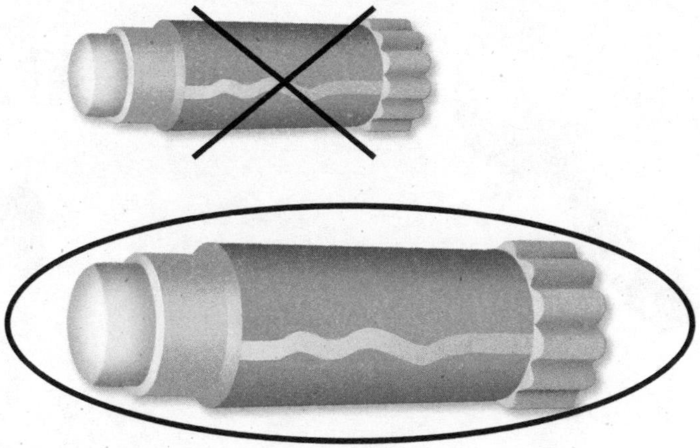

1

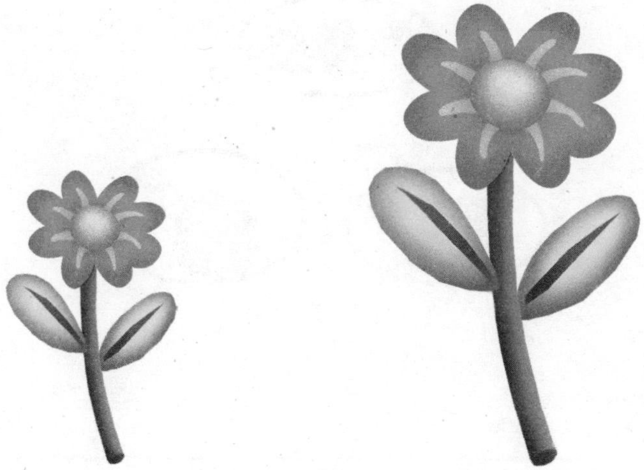

Set B

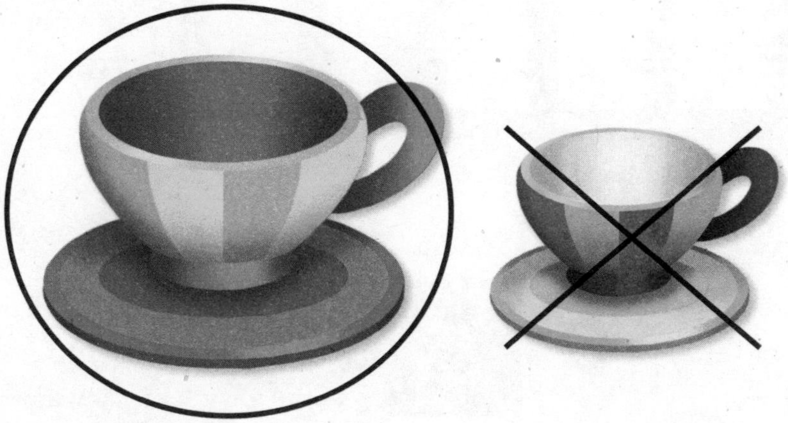

2

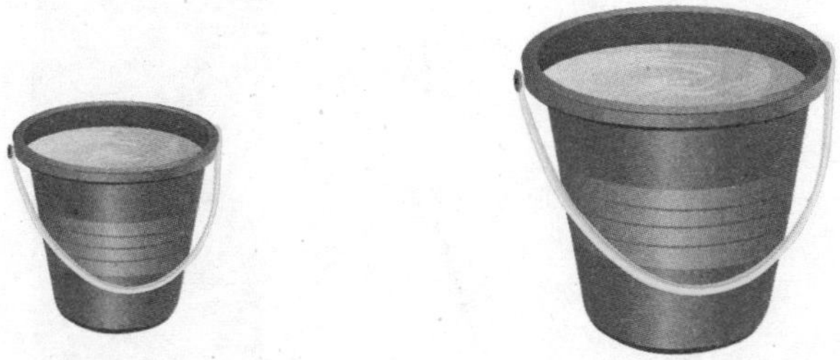

Directions Have students: 1 draw a circle around the taller flower and mark an X on the shorter flower; 2 draw a circle around the bucket that contains more water, and then mark an X on the bucket that contains less water.

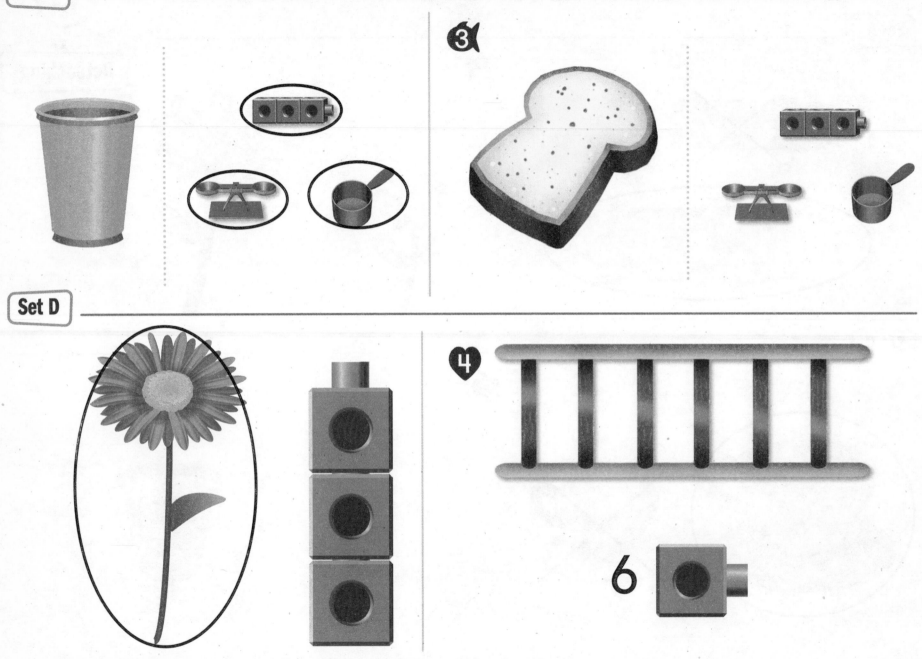

Set D

Directions Have students: ❸ look at the object on the left and identify the attributes that can be measured. Then have students draw a circle around the tool(s) that could be used to tell about those attributes; ❹ make a cube train with the number of cubes shown, compare the length of the cube train to the object, and then draw a circle around the one that is longer.

Name _____

Ⓐ
Ⓑ
Ⓒ
Ⓓ

Ⓐ
Ⓑ
Ⓒ
Ⓓ

3

4

Directions Have students mark the best answer. **1** Which object is shorter than the object on the left but longer than the object on the right? **2** Which object holds less than the other objects? **3** Mark the three objects that can be measured with the tool shown. **4** Have students draw an object that is taller than the toy car, but shorter than the lamp.

Topic 14 | Assessment Practice   five hundred seventy-seven **577**

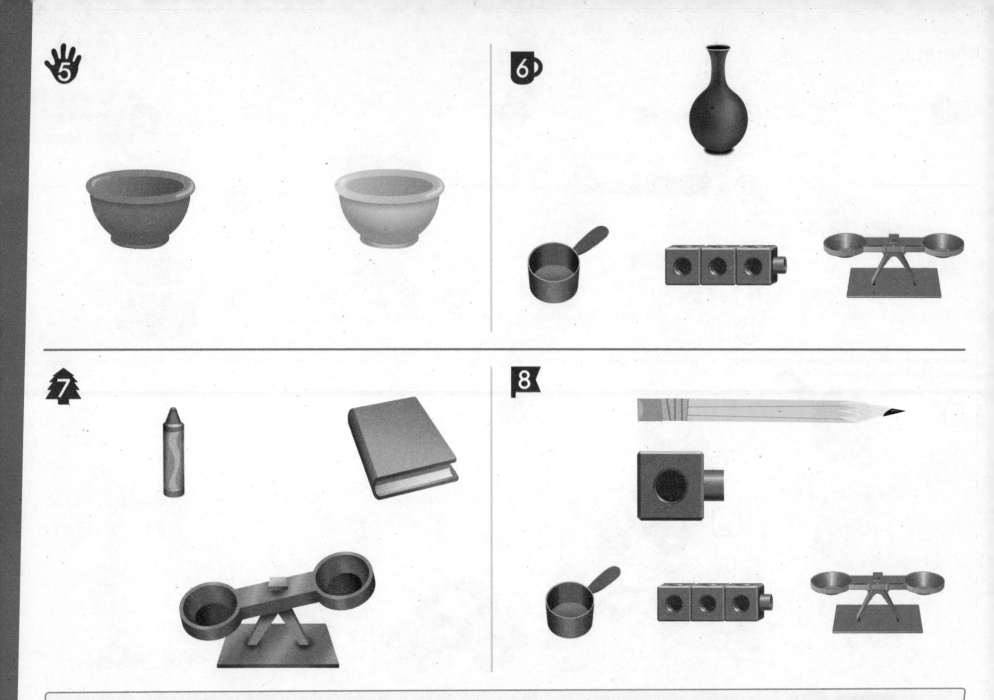

Directions Have students: ✋ draw a circle around the container that holds more, or underline each of the containers if they hold the same amount; ☕ look at the object and identify the attributes that can be measured. Then have them draw a circle around the tool(s) that can be used to measure capacity. 🌲 compare the objects, and then match the heavier object to the lower side of the scale and the lighter object to the higher side of the scale; 🚩 look at the 2 objects. Circle the object that is heavier, or underline both objects if they are the same weight. Then circle the tool that can be used to tell about the weights of the objects.

   Topic 14 | Assessment Practice

Name _____

 1

2

3

Directions **Time for Dinner!** Say: *Teddy helps his father make dinner. They use different things in the kitchen.* Have students: ⬆ look at the fork and the spoon, and then draw a circle around the longer object and mark an X on the shorter object; ② look at the yellow cup and the red cup, and then mark an X on the cup that holds less or underline the cups if they hold the same amount. Then draw a container that would hold more than the red cup; ③ look at the turkey and the corn, and then draw a circle around the heavier object or underline the objects if they have the same weight. Then draw an object that would weigh less than the corn.

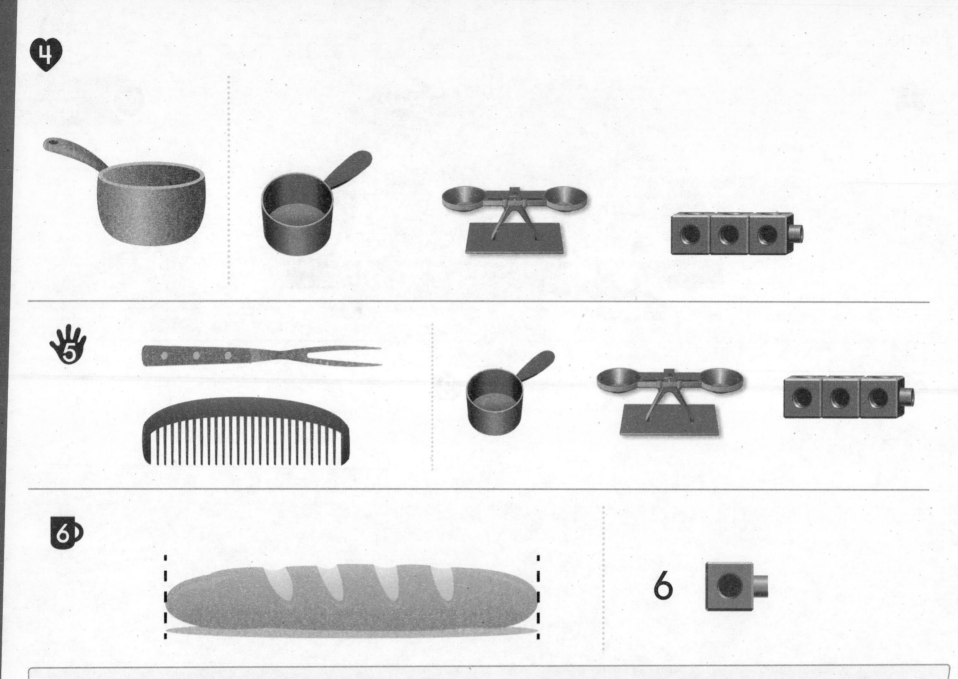

♥ 4

🖐 5

☕ 6

6

Directions ♥ Say: *Teddy and his father will use this pan. What attributes could you measure with the pan?* Have students draw a circle around the tool(s) that could be used to tell about those attributes. 🖐 Have students look at the 2 objects and circle the one that is longer, or underline both objects if they are the same length. Then have them circle the tool that can be used to tell about the lengths of the objects.
☕ Say: *Teddy and his father will eat this bread for dinner.* Have students make a cube train with the number of cubes shown and draw the cube train. Have them compare the length of the cube train to the bread, and then draw a circle around the object that is longer.

 Topic 14 | Performance Task

enVision Mathematics
Common Core

Photographs

Every effort has been made to secure permission and provide appropriate credit for photographic material. The publisher deeply regrets any omission and pledges to correct errors called to its attention in subsequent editions.

Unless otherwise acknowledged, all photographs are the property of Savvas Learning Company LLC.

Photo locators denoted as follows: Top (T), Center (C), Bottom (B), Left (L), Right (R), Background (Bkgd)

1 Jorge Salcedo/Shutterstock; **3** (T) Leighton Photography & Imaging/Shutterstock, (C) FatCamera/iStock/Getty Images, (B) Amy Cicconi/Alamy Stock Photo; **4** (Bkgrd) Rawpixel/Shutterstock, (L) Peacorx/Shutterstock, (R) Yulia Sverdlova/Shutterstock; **57** (L) Evgeny Murtola/Shutterstock, (R) 2rut/Shutterstock; **59** (T) Aleksey Stemmer/Shutterstock, (B) Pedro Turrini Neto/Shutterstock; **60** (T) Loan Florin Cnejevici/123RF, (B) KPG_Payless/Shutterstock; **89** Michal Kolodziejczyk/Fotolia; **91** (T) Carterdayne/E+/Getty Images, (C) Ssuaphotos/Shutterstock, (B) Cdwheatley/iStock/Getty Images; **92** (Bkgrd) Owen Franken/Alamy Stock Photo, Evgeny Karandaev/Shutterstock; **137** James Insogna/Fotolia; **139** (T) LightField Studios/Shutterstock, (B) Daniel Reiter/Alamy Stock Photo; **140** (T) Dmitro2009/Shutterstock, (B) Ian Dagnall/Alamy Stock Photo; **169** Christopher Elwell/Shutterstock; **171** (T) Yui/Shutterstock, (C) Monkey Business Images/Shutterstock, (B) Ted Foxx/Alamy Stock Photo; **172** (Bkgrd) Best dog photo/Shutterstock, Creative Stock Exchange/Shutterstock; **197** Tankist276/Shutterstock; **199** (T) Frank Krahmer/Radius Images/Getty Images, (B) Sean Pavone/Shutterstock; **200** (T) Wisanu_nuu/Shutterstock, (B) Phonix_a Pk.sarote/Shutterstock;

245 Somdul/Shutterstock; **247** (T) Helen Marsden christmassowhite/DigitalVision/Getty Images, (C) 21singha/Shutterstock, (B) Engel Ching/Alamy Stock Photo; **248** (Bkgrd) Leonori/Shutterstock, Gts/Shutterstock, Sarawut Aiemsinsuk/Shutterstock; **289** Winai Tepsuttinun/Shutterstock; **291** (T) Chesh/Alamy Stock Photo, (B) Irina Fischer/Shutterstock; **292** (T) Vovan/Shutterstock, (B) Ron Zmiri/Shutterstock; **345** Panda3800/Shutterstock; **347** (T) Pixpack/123RF, (C) Delpixel/Shutterstock, (B) Dobermaraner/Shutterstock; **348** (Bkgrd) 5second/123RF, Elena Zajchikova/Shutterstock; **385** Turbojet/Shutterstock; **387** (T) Oliveromg/Shutterstock (B) Daniel Mortell/123RF; **388** (T) Inna Reznik/Shutterstock (B) Robert F. Leahy/Shutterstock; **429** Andrey Pavlov/Shutterstock; **431** (T) Nattawat Kaewjirasit/Shutterstock, (C) Africa Studio/Shutterstock, (B) Evru/Shutterstock; **432** (Bkgrd) Anatoli Styf/Shutterstock, Romsvetnik/Shutterstock; **461** Eugene Sergeev/Shutterstock; **463** (T) Robert McGouey/Alamy Stock Photo, (B) ESB Professional/Shutterstock; **464** (T) Olga Ezdakova/Shutterstock, (B) Milena Ugrinova/Shutterstock; **505** Michael Flippo/Fotolia; **507** (T) Monkey Business Images/Shutterstock, (C) Africa Studio/Shutterstock, (B) Stanislav Samoylik/Shutterstock; **508** (Bkgrd) Tomertu/123RF, Berke/Shutterstock; **545** Singkham/Shutterstock; **547** (T) Jean-Paul Chassenet/123RF, (B) Guy Bell/REX/Shutterstock; **548** (T) Wavebreakmediamicro/123RF, (B) Giannimarchetti/Shutterstock.